PREDICTION TECHNIQUES FOR MARKETING PLANNERS

ABP Marketing Library
Editors
Franklin A. Colborn and Aubrey Wilson

Prediction Techniques for Marketing Planners

The practical application of
forecasting methods to business problems

COLIN PEARCE

A HALSTED PRESS BOOK

JOHN WILEY & SONS
New York

English language edition: except U.S.A.
Published by
Associated Business Programmes Ltd
17 Buckingham Gate
London SW1

Published in the U.S.A.
by Halsted Press, a Division
of John Wiley & Sons, Inc.
New York

First published 1971

Pearce, Colin.
        Prediction techniques for marketing planners.

        "A Halsted Press book."
        Includes bibliographical references.
        1. Sales forecasting.   2. Marketing.
        3. Decision-making.   I. Title.
HF5415.2.P4   1973   658.8'18'0184   73-3324
ISBN 0–470–67470–9

Printed in Great Britain
by Ebenezer Baylis and Son Ltd
The Trinity Press, Worcester, and London

Contents

Illustrations

Introduction

The object of this book is to illustrate how business problems in general and marketing problems in particular, may be tackled in a probabilistic manner. In general, the situation which faces the business man is the selection of one alternative or subset of alternatives from a large number of possible alternatives, at a time when the outcome of his selection is not known with certainty. This is essentially the decision making process, and its precise nature is determined by the problem itself and the constraints which are imposed on the decision maker.

To expand this statement it is important to recognise that it is the problem that generates an information need. If sufficient information is available, and obtainable at reasonable cost, to determine with a very high degree of probability which of several alternative events will occur, then it may be relatively easy to select that decision alternative which is most favourable to the desired objective.

In most practical marketing problems there is usually some information readily available at negligible cost. If this is sufficient, then the problem of the worth of further data does not arise. In many cases, however, the quantity or nature of the existing information is insufficient to allow the proper choice to be made between the available alternatives. Hence it is necessary to consider what further knowledge is required and to weigh the cost of obtaining this information against the consequential cost of selecting the wrong alternative. There will also be some cases where further information is totally unavailable.

It is obvious, therefore, that a degree of uncertainty will be present in the decision process. This uncertainty arises from the lack of clear information about which of various events will occur. It is at this point in the decision process that prediction comes into action.

Suppose a situation exists that if x units are produced and if about x units are demanded, this will be very favourable to the Company. To assess the situation it is necessary to forecast demand for the product. If the probability that demand will exceed x is high, then the risk of over-producing is small, if exactly x units are made. In other words, the Company has a high probability of selling all its produce. The other side of the same coin is that an opportunity of selling more than x may be lost. The decision may rest upon weighing the expected opportunity loss against the cost of failing to sell all that is produced.

This simple situation implicitly pinpoints the aspects of a typical marketing problem which for convenience of examination may be divided into a number of stages. These are shown in detail on pages 58 and 59.

Brief Review by Chapter

The opening chapter is a general introduction to the problem areas within the marketing framework, where prediction is important. It demonstrates the dependence of successful marketing on successful prediction and indicates some of the limitations involved. One section is devoted to the logical processes involved in forecasting. The last two parts discuss the information requirements which are generated by the problem and attempts to explain how these interact.

The second chapter deals with *information*, with discussions on the methods available of evaluating the worth of better knowledge and how to set about acquiring it. The question of *worth* is extremely important and will arise in several chapters. Also in this chapter are special sections on market research and feedback. Feedback is specially important since it should be the core of the market intelligence system.

The third chapter deals with forecasting methodology commencing with the simplest approaches—i.e. estimates made by salesmen and market experts. Although there are certain obvious weaknesses in this type of predicting, it is hoped that it will be shown that expert judgement has an important role to play in the predictive process. Before this role is considered in detail, the uses, abuses and limitations of time series analysis is considered and some of the simpler methodology is included.

In chapter 4 the econometric approach to predicting is introduced and this leads to the formulation of descriptive non-mathematical models. Although econometrics is in a sense a relatively young discipline and historically is concerned with establishing relationships between economic variables, the philosophy is essentially that of scientific methodology. It is, however, not practical to discuss here more than some of the basic ideas and methods, as the book is not aimed at the mathematical reader. The methods discussed show how causative factors are isolated and their effects measured on a variable of interest. In some cases these relationships may be expressed in a non-mathematical form.

The logic of systematic and consistent decision making is discussed in greater depth in chapter 5. Special emphasis is given to the role of probability theory and the assessment and meaning of *risk*. In this chapter, the expected monetary value approach is discussed, together with the main limitations of the criterion—that is, the concept of risk.

Before considering the problems of decision making, it is necessary to consider in detail the underlying principles involved. Chapter 6 attempts to do this by considering probability theory in greater detail and by emphasising the role of hypothesis formulation. In these sections, relevant definitions are given together with the basic laws of probability and it is shown that the decision tree technique is valuable in the analysis of business problems.

Chapter 7 provides a detailed case study of an actual disinvestment situation which required market and pricing problems to be resolved. The chapter is divided into eight sections which correspond with the stages of the situation and some mention is made of the compromises that have to be made in dealing with practical problems. The approach reflects much of the material given in chapters 1 to 6 but it goes further and shows the practical application of parts of this material to a specific problem.

In chapter 8 a second detailed case study is discussed. This is an acquisition study which may be considered in a sense as a typical investment problem. Again, the chapter provides a practical illustration of the broad approach used to tackle questions as they arise.

Chapter 9 is an attempt to combine the material in chapters 1 to 8 into a integrated system within which marketing problems are considered. Only at this point can an attempt be made to answer the question as to what constitutes a good 'decision', and whether the test of a decision lies in the result or whether the real issue is the examination of the logical processes involved quite independently of the result.

In chapter 10 the first section is concerned with the practical application of scientific methodology to general business problems. The last section indicates some ways in which management science may become of increasing importance not only to the business world, but also to society as a whole.

CHAPTER 1

The Dependence of Successful Marketing on Successful Forecasting

REASONS FOR FORECASTING, USES AND LIMITATIONS

The fundamental reason why predicting is necessary is because every organisation generates problems and in general the state of knowledge of the decision maker is uncertain.

To understand how problems are generated it is necessary to realise that the basic purpose of any organisation is to direct the organised effort to some common goal or set of goals. In business, these goals are generally concerned with profitability but others, such as sociological, are not excluded. The mere existence of a set of targets and policies is sufficient to allow problems to arise.

In practice the birth of a problem occurs because of the interaction of either internal or external factors with company policies. External factors may be caused by an internal policy, for example change in price may affect demand, or may occur quite independently, for example change in bank rate is not caused by an individual company. The fact that an external factor is independent in origin indicates that no control can be exerted over its occurrence. This may very well be true, but from past experience of such changes it is often possible to make realistic predictions about the effects such a change will have on the company's operations.

The problems which a company will have to face are really implicit in the policies of the company. It may, however, require some catalytic action to occur, such as change in the external environment, before the problem becomes a fact. Moreover, it is not only changes in the external circumstances, but changes within the organisation which may be important.

If a problem arises or is foreseen then this implies that some decision will have to be made. Such decision making is fundamental to any business organisation and in most cases it occurs under conditions of uncertainty. If the decision is necessary and insufficient information is available, or obtainable, to be certain which of several events will occur, then the best approach is to consider the probability of each possible occurrence and its consequent effect, if a particular decision alternative[1] is chosen. This is the purpose of prediction.

As an example consider the following situation:

The decision maker must choose between the following alternative actions

    (a) do not increase production;
    (b) increase production by say 10 per cent;
    (c) increase production by say 50 per cent.

Suppose his present state of knowledge is that production is far from capacity, but that he knows nothing at all of the market conditions. In this case he is likely to choose the first alternative—no increase—since increasing production capacity may be a costly operation and there is no evidence to suggest it is necessary. His implicit, if not explicit, thinking is that there is a high probability that present output will cope with future demand. If from past experience he considers the probability of this to be 95 per cent likely then the implication is that his decision will be right on average nineteen times out of twenty. There is, however, a risk, a 5 per cent chance in this case, that he is wrong and depending on the circumstances he may or may not be prepared to take this risk. His actual decision should depend on the costs involved if the decision turned out to be wrong. If these consequential costs are very high, even though the probability of them occurring is low, the expected loss of business or goodwill, may exceed the cost of increased production.

The above simple example was designed to show how the decision maker is concerned with evaluating the consequences of each of his possible acts in the light of the real state of

[1] Decision alternative is defined as a single terminal act which may be selected from some set of acts.

nature.[1] In other words, it is necessary to consider the probabilities of each situation occurring, that is static demand or increased demand levels, and make his decision on the basis of the effect of each situation on his possible acts and associated probabilities. In the business situation where the profit motive is generally the main criterion these effects need to be considered in terms of costs and profits associated with each act and each state of nature.

The evaluation of the consequences of his choosing a given decision alternative, depends very heavily upon his ability to predict the probabilities of the various alternative states, that is high or low levels of demand. He may, as in the above example, rely on his past experience or he may initiate a market investigation. If the decision must be made quickly or the cost of the market investigation is too high, then he may be perfectly justified in relying on his own personal assessment, but there are many cases where he would be very wrong in doing so.

It is emphasised that the real basis of successful marketing decision making is the ability to predict with known precision. In this context, precision is the assessment of the probability with which events may or may not occur.

It should be noted that a decision maker, without making a demand forecast, could still make a correct decision purely by chance. However, consistent decision[2] making depends on consistent prediction[3] and a systematic approach to the problem in hand using all available applicable information.

The information obtained from a forecasting system is relevant directly or indirectly to most marketing problems. In constructing a system a greater understanding of the market

[1] State of nature is called 'state of the world' by Howard Raiffa and Robert Schaiffer in 'Applied Statistical Decision Theory'—page 3. The decision maker believes that the consequences of choosing a specific act depend on some 'state of nature which he cannot predict with certainty'.
[2] Consistent decision making refers to the manner in which a decision alternative is selected—not that the outcome will always be favourable or correct.
[3] Consistent prediction means forecasting on a logical basis using all available information.

factors at work is often obtained. This knowledge by itself will often aid the decision maker.

PROBLEM AREAS REQUIRING SUCCESSFUL PREDICTION

In the previous section some consideration was given to the genesis of a problem and it was observed that in general the problem is implicit in the situation. In ideal circumstances it may be possible to predict from detailed knowledge of the organisation and its policies the problems which might arise if certain events occur. Even in the practical non-ideal situation some effort should be made to foresee the occurrence of the more important problems that are likely to occur and how the predictive processes are used, when they do. It is not concerned with estimating the probability that a given problem will arise, but with the procedure required, given that it has occurred. The following constitutes the major problem areas where the marketing decision maker may be involved either directly or indirectly.

Inventory Control of Raw Materials, Components and Finished Products

Forecasting demand levels plays an important role in most problems under the above heading. This role is demonstrated by an example where failure to make accurate predictions could lead to wrong decisions and high consequential costs.

The example concerns the case of a manufacturer of complex equipment which requires bought-in components. One component in particular is critical in the sense that the manufacturer of the equipment cannot continue until it is incorporated and further, no substitution can be made. If this component is out of stock a delay period of over two months is likely to occur before the stock is replenished.

The problem is essentially to decide how many of these components the manufacturer should keep in stock, for the consequences of running out could be a disastrous loss in production. If demand for the product can be predicted with calculable probability then sufficient components can be stocked to ensure that there will be no hold up with a pre-determined probability. In other words, if the acceptable risk of running out in a given period of time is one in ten thousand, then sufficient are stocked to ensure that the probability of this event occurring is less than one in ten thousand.

Under some circumstances, calculation may show that the cost of keeping so many items in stock is prohibitive. If this is the case, a compromise must be reached between the risk of losing production and consequent costs involved, and the cost of stocking the components. The way in which this type of decision may be made will be discussed later. Here the interest is only in the role which the demand-forecasts and associated probability-estimates play in the decision process.

Manpower Requirements and Associated Problems

Demand-level forecasts have direct application to problems such as labour relations, wages, hours of work and other conditions of employment. In addition to relations between demand levels and manpower problems, it is also necessary to predict the level of supply of skilled labour or specialists which will be available at a given point in time.

The typical situation may be the choice between not increasing the labour force or increasing it by various amounts. This is similar to the previous problem on page 16, and the importance of good demand predictions cannot be over-emphasised.

A less obvious example is where a manufacturer is considering allocating a large R. & D. budget for the development of a highly sophisticated product. The full scale production of this product may require a specialist skill either in design or the production process itself. It is, therefore, of the utmost importance to determine whether there is a sufficient supply of personnel possessing this skill to permit full production. If there is not, then it is necessary to consider whether sufficient may be obtained. Although this problem involves manpower predictions, it is actually an investment problem—investment in R. & D., and as such should be considered at the investment decision stage.

Distribution Problems

The type of question to be answered here such as warehouse sitings, size and nature of fleet and many others, depend very much on demand levels and patterns of demand.

As an example, consider the case of a manufacturer of a product with pronounced seasonal demand patterns. In this case, the cost of maintaining a fleet sufficient to deal with peak demand may be prohibitive and other solutions must be sought. The choice may be between employing outside distributors, levelling off production throughout the year and maintaining high stocks, or sub-contracting work at peak demand times. To make this choice it is necessary to know the costs involved in each case and to be able to predict when demand level peaks will occur and also their magnitude. Although only three decision alternatives have been explicitly mentioned, in most cases many more exist. In this particular case the decision maker might also consider any combination of the three alternatives, or he might consider others—for example by offering high discounts during the periods of low demand and by trying to persuade customers that they can avoid the risk of being disappointed by keeping stocks themselves.

Price and Discount Policies

There are many marketing problems under this heading which require successful predictions.

A typical case is where a manufacturer's production capacity is reaching its limit. He may be faced with the choice between quoting longer delivery dates, rejecting orders outright, not to tender at all or to increase prices in selected cases to decrease his probability of getting orders. Similarly if production is far from capacity and orders are required urgently then a reduction in price may increase his probability of success. These problems may require either or both of demand forecasting and estimating the price/demand elasticity of the product.

Pricing policies are often determinants of demand. Hence although the policies may be considered in the light of demand forecasts it is essential to attempt to understand the effects such policies have on demand. In some markets where demand is relatively insensitive to price, these problems are less important.

Capital Expenditure and Investment Analysis

In the typical acquisition study, for example, the decision whether to invest depends upon the profits which the acquired company is expected to make during a specified period. To estimate this profitability it may be necessary to make demand forecasts for the products they make. From these demand forecasts conditional forecasts of profitability may be made. This type of study can be a complex business and forecasting profitability is in general the most important part.

The preceding areas constitute a very incomplete list of problems requiring prediction.

THE LOGIC OF FORECASTING

The term prediction usually refers to any situation where it is not known with certainty which of several events have occurred or will occur. Forecasting is often used in a special sense— predicting future events. In this text both terms may be regarded as synonymous.

While the idea of reaching a conclusion about some past event is generally acceptable, the concept of predicting some future event is often regarded with suspicion and mistrust. In one sense this mistrust is well founded but in a more important sense it is illogical.

If a crime has been committed, the evidence is scrutinised and may result in a charge being made. The person who is charged appears before a jury and this jury assesses the evidence in as objective a manner as the jury members are able. From the evidence, a conclusion is reached as to whether the man actually committed the crime or not. In most cases this conclusion is really equivalent to the jury saying that there is a very high probability that he did. Seldom can they be absolutely certain, even if absolute certainty were ever attainable, and therefore, there must always be a risk that the wrong conclusion (decision) was made. In fact there are cases of criminals convicted of extreme crimes after long and deliberate consideration of the facts, who are pardoned later because further information becomes available.

There are two main reasons why the idea of predicting a future event is not always acceptable. The first is because of the time element involved and the second because of the poor performance of most forecasters in the past (except perhaps prophets!). In relation to the time element, when a crime has been committed it is at least known that it occurred and the popular concept is not of predicting the criminal responsible but proving him guilty. In fact predicting and proving, or rather attempting to prove, are more or less the same thing. When a future event is considered, a whole range of irrationality arises. Yet it is known that next Easter will fall on one of the days of the week and hence the probability of it falling on a Sunday is one in seven. This is a prediction about a future event. If this prediction were insufficient a clergyman might be asked for his expert opinion. If he also stated Sunday then the probability of it happening may be increased to 99 per cent likely. If this is not good enough then consulting next year's calendar may permit the probability to be revised to say 99·999 per cent—there is a small chance of the calendar being wrong.

In this example, the procedure is essentially the same as attempting to prove a man guilty of a crime. That is that the evidence is considered and a judgement made about the probability involved. If this probability is too low then further information is sought until the case is 'proven'.

The second reason why forecasting is sometimes unacceptable is more difficult to rationalise. This reason is that in past human experience predictions have been left to witches and fortune tellers on the one hand and scientists on the other. The former have tended to rely upon superstition and the stars and their methods have been very suspect. The scientists have been more objective and cautious about their predictions and certainly keener to test the hypotheses involved. They have suffered, however, until lately of being an extremely small minority group and further their scientific methods were not well understood.

Although no prediction can be made with certainty, there are still many cases where the probability of an event occurring is extremely high. These cases will generally be taken as exact knowledge in the decision processes, whereas those events with smaller probabilities of occurring will be considered predictions. If no evidence is available at all about a given event then it is not known whether it will occur or not—that is the probability of occurring is 0·5. However slight the evidence, it may be used to amend this probability. There are methods available for making these revisions in a systematic, logical and consistent manner. If a higher probability is required then further information, if available, must be sought.

The predictive process concerns the gathering of evidence so that a conclusion about the happening of some future or past event can be drawn. This conclusion is dependent upon the nature of the problem and the time and cost constraints involved.

INFORMATION AND PREDICTION REQUIREMENTS GENERATED BY THE PROBLEM

When a problem occurs, this invariably requires the selection of a decision alternative for its solution and, to permit rational selection, certain information is required and predictions must be made. It is necessary to mention at this stage, the main purpose of taking a consistent and systematic approach to decision making. The reason is essentially so that the subjective element in the process can be reduced and at the same time so that the objective part may be increased. This is naturally subject to cost and time restrictions.

The essential requirements are sufficient applicable and reliable information, the use of probability theory and expert judgement. In this section of the chapter only the first requirement is considered in detail with some reference to the predictive needs. There is a fundamental quality which the decision maker must possess if he is to make maximum contribution to his organisation's activities. This is an analytical ability which enables him to understand the nature of the problem in hand; to be able to set down all the possible actions which may be taken, that is decision alternatives; to be able to consider all the possible events that may occur and finally to consider the results of making a particular decision when a specific event or set of events occurs. If the decision maker has this ability then he will be in the position to judge what information is required and the techniques of decision theory should enable him to judge the worth of obtaining this information.

The type of information required depends upon the problem. Two examples are given here to illustrate this. If there is too high a proportion of defectives being produced in a factory, then this requires different information from the case where the sales manager must decide whether to increase his sales force. In the first situation, the problem arises perhaps because of a high level of complaints from customers, some loss of business, consequential costs of making and delivering replacements or in a variety of other ways. Clearly the first information required is an estimate of the cost or potential cost, including loss of reputation—a long term cost, to the company. Some of these costs may be precisely estimated while others may not. Where estimates are made, for example, by group discussion by market experts, these should be used with estimates of the probabilities with which the values are likely to occur.

Similarly the cost involved in selecting each alternative will need to be estimated. In the example chosen machine replacements may decrease the occurrence of defective units to a tolerable level with an extremely high probability, whereas the employment of an inspector may make the same reduction with a lower probability. Since the costs are likely to vary between the alternatives this needs to be considered in the decision process.

In the sales manager example, the information required is demand levels and consequent profit levels, and the cost of increasing the sales force. The demand and profit levels will in general be predictions and the probability that demand exceeds various levels would need to be calculated. The costs of increasing the sales force are calculable with a very high degree of probability and may be regarded as certain knowledge. The cost estimates and predictions are used directly in the decision process.

These two examples demonstrate the widely differing information requirements of two separate problems. This difference is in the nature of the information—in one case demand levels and salesman's salaries; in the other case costs of producing defective components and costs of remedying the situation. Such differences in the information need is relatively unimportant, because its nature will be evident from the clear formulation of the problem. The real information needs are those of costs involved in undertaking particular actions and estimates of the probabilities with which particular events will occur. These two requirements are necessary conditions for decision making to be made on a rational and systematic basis and are fundamental to all decision processes. One further point is that costs need not necessarily be measured in financial terms alone. A sound financial proposition may be rejected in favour of a less beneficial one if for example the former conflicted in some way with sociological or other beliefs of the board. With the profit motive so powerful, this type of situation is not so likely to occur, unless there is some chance of, say, prosecution—but this case may be considered in terms of financial loss.

THE INTERACTION OF INFORMATION AND PREDICTION

In general, decision making takes place in a dynamic environment. If it were possible to make a particular decision at any point over a period of time during which applicable information is collected, then in many cases the additional knowledge at the end of the period will permit better decision making. Ideally then, it is necessary to calculate the cost of making incorrect decisions at each point in this period and weigh this cost against the cost involved in gathering more information or in delaying the decision.

In practice this approach is unnecessary for many problems because the difference in costs involved are small. In a major marketing exercise for a new product, this approach may be well worthwhile. For this situation the use of Bayesian[1] methods in assessing the value of further information offers considerable potential. Some consideration will be given to the relevant methods in later chapters.

As a graphic summary of some of the material in this chapter and to demonstrate especially the interaction between information and predictive needs of a problem, *Figure 1* shows the steps in the decision process.

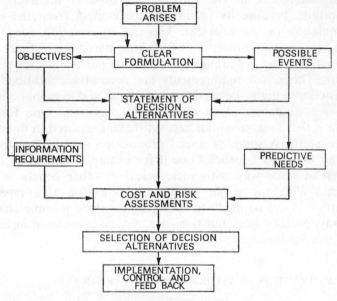

Figure 1

INTERACTION BETWEEN INFORMATION AND FORECASTING
REQUIREMENTS IN THE DECISION PROCESS

[1] Bayesian methods encompass the so called inverse probability in inductive reason. This sort of reasoning assumes that something is certain to happen in the future to evaluate the consequences of making a decision now. Chapter 6 discusses the Bayesian approach.

Check List

1. Have the company's objectives been formulated in writing?

2. Were all the managers concerned with implementing the objectives invited to comment at the draft stage?

3. Have the final objectives now been circulated to all managers whose decisions will affect implementation?

4. Have the problems which may arise in attaining the objectives been formulated and written down?
   (*a*) short-term problems
   (*b*) medium-term problems
   (*c*) long-term problems

5. Have the alternative choices facing the company been set down?

6. Does the proposed solution of any problem appear to be constrained by or conflict with corporate objectives?

7. Has a survey been made of the information required before work on the problems can begin?

8. Has the cost of obtaining this information been calculated?

9. Have the events which may occur been listed?

10. Has the probability of their happening been calculated and evaluated in each case?

11. Has the cost of choosing given alternatives been calculated for each of them?

12. Have the consequences of choosing specified courses of action been calculated?

The chapters that follow are designed to contribute to seeking a more accurate answer than 'yes' to each of the above questions.

REFERENCES

'Statistical methods of inventory control', W. C. Henshaw, *The Statistician*, Vol. 15, No. 1, 1965

'The statistical analysis of stock movements in the man-made fibre industry', J. M. Low, *The Statistician*, Vol. 14, No. 1, 1964

Planning and Problem Solving in Marketing, W. Alderson and P. E. Green (Homewood Ill.; Irwin), 1964

'Risk analysis in capital investment', D. B. Hertz, *Harvard Business Review*, 42, 1964

The Logic of Decision, R. C. Jeffrey, New York and London, McGraw-Hill, 1965

Problems of Stocks and Storage, Edited by A. J. H. Morrell, London and Edinburgh, Oliver and Boyd, 1967

CHAPTER 2

The Organisation, Control and Use of Information in the Prediction Processes

INFORMATION REQUIREMENTS

In considering the general business problem it is obviously not possible nor practicable to state exact information requirements. This is because such requirements depend essentially upon the specific nature of the particular problem being tackled.

To discuss this topic in a formal manner, only two approaches are possible. These are to consider either specific problems and their specific demands or to attempt to lay down some general ground rules. The approach here is a combination of the two, using examples to illustrate general rules.

Before considering such rules and examples in detail it is vital to understand how the parts of a complete organisation fit together within the overall framework. It is also necessary to appreciate that full synergistic[1] benefits are unlikely to be achieved unless the organisation has a properly designed information system.

The concept used is that a specific function such as marketing may be considered to be a closed system which links into an organisational structure. This concept permits an overall view of the total organisation and the interaction of its separate parts. If information systems are formed on the basis of such an understanding then the following discussion will be relevant to the total organisation as well as its specific parts. Certainly, if proper control is to be maintained then a systematic approach to organisational and marketing needs is essential.

However the marketing function is defined it can readily be

[1] Synergistic benefits—for example rationalising production or distribution by combining two separate businesses so that the total benefit is greater than the sum of the two separate businesses.

viewed as such a closed system within which marketing decisions should be made with reference to corporate strategy. The links should be through the information system.

The total information available to a company may conveniently be classified into two sources—that generated within the company and that which is available from external sources. The principal objective in setting up a rigorous information system is to improve, even to optimise, corporate decision making. This may be achieved by reducing the uncertainty in a given, situation improving the forecasting ability, permitting formal decision procedures to be used, or just learning more from past experience. In practice the aim should be to achieve each of these.

The system should ensure that internally generated information is isolated and allowed to flow to the points where it is required. Externally derived information must be identified and allowed to enter the appropriate stream. There must always be sufficient skilled personnel available to perform intelligence work and research work, in addition to the natural market contacts such as salesmen.

The system must not only provide the means for information to circulate but must ensure that proper analysis and interpretation are carried out.

Ensuring that adequate circulation and analysis is achieved is not enough. If the knowledge is not properly used then the system is wasted. Hence there must be a formal control system. This should be constructed around records on how the system was used in a specific case and what outcome of the decision was observed. Properly conducted this should provide all the feedback required for the corporation to learn effectively from its experience.

Additionally there are two properties which should be sought. The first relates to the 'sin of ommission'. This really means that the occurrence of a specific rare event could have disastrous consequences or the converse. Hence the ideal system would identify the possibility of all such rare events, that is those events with low probabilities of occurring, and some attempt must be made to assess the affects of their occurring. This could even lead to the Utopian state where ready-made strategy packets are taken off the shelf as and when required.

The second desirable property is that some mechanism should exist to attempt to calculate the worth of future information against the cost of obtaining it, in a given situation. This means trying to assess the cost of making a wrong decision. For example, choosing to eat at one of two restaurants of unknown virtues would in general hardly warrant buying prior information for if the one chosen produced tasteless food the loss would not be great. However, for a business lunch it is easy to think of circumstances where it would be advisable to minimise the risk of dissatifaction by making prior enquiries.

The simpler the organisation the easier it is to operate a system which satisfies the preceding requirements. The converse is also true although the computer hardware currently available can enable a reasonably comprehensive system to function well. For the large conglomerate a well designed system is required to cope with the complex issues which arise.

To demonstrate the relevance of formal information systems a trivial situation is chosen in the example which follows. It is useful to take an extremely simple case for illustrative purposes.

Simple Example

One of the simplest business situations must be that of the self-employed decorator, operating at a time when the demand for his services exceeds his capacity. In this case he has a clearly defined production constraint which he could presumably quantify easily.

If he is reasonably shrewd he may consider strategies other than quoting at a standard rate for whatever business comes his way. He may, for example, consider specialising in one segment of the market—perhaps to work as a sub-contractor to a main building contractor. If he chose this strategy he should be able to assess accurately the likely level of his earnings and he would run little risk of bad debts.

An alternative strategy may be for him to go for the 'luxury' end of the market where margins would probably be higher, but where the risk of bad debts would be greater.

Another alternative may be for him to deal with the small 'cash on the nail' jobs. Margins would be lower but the risk of bad debts would be smaller. He may also take into account the opportunities to minimise his tax payments!

The above constitute the three alternative strategies the business man is prepared to consider. The next question is how he makes his choice and this of course requires information. His internal information requirements are easy to specify as follows

1. *Production*   (*a*) Capacity
                  (*b*) Nature of work he can undertake
                  (*c*) The quality he can produce

2. *Financial*   (*a*) The minimum earnings to give him an acceptable standard of living
                  (*b*) Marginal rates of taxation
                  (*c*) Costs of materials
                  (*d*) Profit margins
                  (*e*) Capital requirements
                  (*f*) Funding requirements—for debts

3. *Administrative capability*
Obviously this is more relevant in the case of working as a sub-contractor.

4. *Personal preferences*
For particular types of work or locations.

It is implicitly assumed that in this example he does not want to expand his business—he only wishes to maximise his earnings, minimise the risks involved and do the work he enjoys. Since he is unlikely to be able to do all three he really wishes to choose the optimal alternative.

His external information needs may be listed as follows

determine whether the market segment can provide him with sufficient work:

determine what margins he is likely to make in each case (possibly from his potential competitors);

determine the level of debtors he is likely to have and the risk of bad debts;

find out whether any of the segments set a premium on any particular skill he has to offer;

determine precisely the nature and quality of work required in each segment;

establish which segment would give him the greatest job satisfaction.

This information will allow him to determine which alternative is likely to yield the best pay-off given that demand continued to exceed supply and that the whole situation was static. Since this, in general, is not even approximately true he may be well advised to consider his problem in a dynamic sense. Essentially this means considering specific events which might happen and trying to assess the affects of these—favourable or otherwise—on his business if they occur. One example could be if he chose the sub-contracting strategy at a time when industrial rationalisation could have an adverse effect on the small trader.

If he were to adopt a rigorous system he would write down all the possible events and endeavour to assess the effect of each one on his operations given that he had chosen a particular alternative. This stage is likely to require further information.

In this simple case the man is the business and hence information flows within the organisation do not exist. He may analyse the information gathered and conclude that a particular strategy is optimal in the financial sense. However, it may be his 'least preferred' case and this may lead him to choose one of the others. The difference between the expected earnings of his choice and that of the optimum is essentially a partial measure of the cost of his preference.

The decorator could obviously change strategy reasonably quickly if market changes warranted it. Hence the assessment of the affects of future events, except in the short-term, are fairly irrelevant. However, for the sake of rigour—and there are many cases where it is essential—it is assumed that once a course of action is chosen it becomes expensive, or takes a long time, to change again.

Having considered the affects of each chance event, the typical small businessman would weigh up the 'pros and cons', probably in his head, and eventually make his decision. As an aside it would be interesting if it were possible to calculate the proportion of successful entrepreneurs who owe their success to the laws of chance.

A more formal approach has some advantages, especially in the more complex situation. This is suggested step by step below

The known quantitative parts of the decision process are written down in a systematic way. The information used to make various estimates should also be shown. This decreases the chance that the decision maker will overlook an important factor or miss a relevant interrelationship. It also provides an opportunity for an independent assessment as well as being a record of the decision making process.

Formal mathematical methods may be used to assess the affects of various events in probabilistic terms and permit expected pay-offs to be calculated. The various methods available should ensure that all the information gathered is used and ought to demonstrate what further information is required. If further information is obtainable formal or informal methods may be used to decide whether it is worth the extra costs or time involved.

Perhaps the most important point of all is the built-in learning system. Whether the actual outcome is favourable or not, the process can be re-examined retrospectively in an attempt to learn as much as possible from each situation. For example if such an examination revealed faulty logic or even numerical inaccuracies it is possible that steps may be taken to prevent them recurring. Following this routine should ensure that the organisation improves its decision making.

Some mention should be made of the formal methods which may be used in decision making, although this anticipates topics which receive considerable attention later.

One method is to construct a decision tree which depicts all the alternatives open to the decision maker. In a decision tree diagram, an example of which is *Figure 2*, below, the alternatives are denoted by squares.

The diagram should also show all the possible events which may occur and the consequences of their occurring are usually shown as pay-offs. This means that if a particular alternative is chosen and a specific event occurs then there is a single outcome. In the diagram the events are usually represented by circles.

The decision tree is a technique for determining the best decision to make in terms of some financial pay-off, given that the various outcomes and their probabilities of occurring can be estimated. However, if the method is to approach reality it is necessary to make some statement about the risk involved in each alternative. This is necessarily a subjective assessment

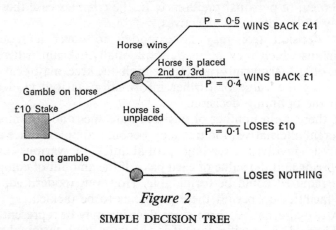

Figure 2

SIMPLE DECISION TREE

Personal Preference

The punter is prepared to risk £10 on a 'good bet' but is not prepared to accept more than a 10 per cent chance of losing the whole £10. In this case both conditions are satisfied, if his estimates of the probabilities involved are correct.

Note: Although the odds offered are 6 to 1—that is the bookies believe the probability of the horse winning is $\frac{1}{6}$th, the punter believes the probability involved to be $\frac{1}{2}$.

although it should be based on calculated probabilities. For example, if the probability of at least breaking even in operating a new plant within one year is 90 per cent, then this implies that there is a 10 per cent chance of failure. Risk is inextricably tied up with probability, in this case, risk of failure, but the concept goes beyond probability. For example, if the loss, if it occurred, were very small relative to total resources then the risk may be considered insignificant. However if it were a business where the entrepreneur had mortgaged everything he possessed, then failure could bankrupt him. This may be too big a risk to take, even though the probability of the entrepreneur failing is equal to the case where cost of failure is insignificant.

The expected return from the first alternative (i.e. to gamble) is

$$0.5 \times 41 + 0.4 \times 1 - 0.1 \times 10 = 20.5 + .4 - 1 = £19.9$$

In addition to statements of risk it is advisable to have a statement of personal preference. In the complex case these are likely to be company objectives.

A decision tree may be extended to cover a series of decisions which may be made sequentially.[1] Again, where the cost of gathering information is high the tree may deal with assessing the value of further information as well as dealing with the optimum decision.

If there are a number of possible outcomes and a number of different alternatives the tree may become complex. Since a full analysis involves assessing probabilities of various events occurring and the value of each pay-off the amount of computation required could be formidable. However, modern computing facilities do permit these problems to be tackled.

A two-alternative, three-event decision may be represented as in *Figure 2*. A specific pay-off is shown at each terminal point and probabilities are indicated above the event circles. In the right hand column personal preferences and risk statements are made. If subjective probability estimates are made then the reasons should be shown in each case.

Figure 2 represents the punter who can get 6 to 1 odds on a

---

[1] Sequentially here means that the decision maker may be faced with a series of alternatives at different points in time.

horse which he believes has an even chance of winning and a
90 per cent chance of being in the first three. The tree shows
the three events which may occur and the calculated pay-off
and the two-alternative decisions.

It is interesting to note that the gambler may not be prepared
to risk £10. He could calculate his expected returns on decreasing capital outlay until he reached an alternative which he
considered acceptable.

OBTAINING THE NECESSARY INFORMATION

Some general rules for information requirements have been laid
down and now specific information sources and flow systems
are considered. There are very many sources and ways of
handling and distributing information, only some of which can
be discussed.

Before setting up an information system with specific characteristics, company objectives and the problems that are most
likely to arise must be specified. The marketing information
system must be integrated into the overall system so that all
parts of the total organisation function in a complementary
manner. If it is properly integrated, then it can be examined in
isolation. Before carrying out this examination the meaning of
'the marketing function' needs to be demonstrated by indicating
the business problems which require market information.
These are not necessarily problems which would normally
be termed marketing.

Production Problems
(a) Product changes—i.e. re-design, substitution and reducing
    or increasing the range available.
(b) Plant location—with respect to material availability, market
    and manpower requirements.
(c) Capacity requirements—including product mix.
(d) Inventory control—including raw materials and spares as
    well as finished goods.
(e) Manpower requirements—and how these might change
    with changing products or mix.
(f) Package or batch size—including design.

(*g*) Labour relations, wages and hours.
(*h*) Technological changes—both in manufacturing methods and products.

Sales
(*a*) Market potential—by product market segment including both primary and secondary markets.
(*b*) Defining market areas—i.e. geographical and by industry or user.
(*c*) Distribution methods.
(*d*) Location and selection of distributors if required.
(*e*) Size and organisation of sales force.
(*f*) Sales force control and target setting.
(*g*) Salesmen's training requirements.
(*h*) Salesmen's remuneration methods.
(*i*) Evaluating competitive strengths and weaknesses.
(*j*) Determining customers' preferences and prejudices.
(*k*) Establishing the principal purchasing influences.

Advertising
(*a*) Budget requirements.
(*b*) Distribution of budget—by territory, product and media.
(*c*) Selection of appropriate media.
(*d*) Deciding on the appropriate message.
(*e*) Measuring the impact of advertising.

Financial
(*a*) Working capital requirements.
(*b*) Fixed capital requirements.
(*c*) Appropriate credit policy.
(*d*) Discount policy.
(*e*) Stockholder relations.
(*f*) Pricing and bidding policy.
(*g*) Investment appraisal.
(*h*) Acquisition studies.
(*i*) Inter-firm and inter-industry cross section analysis.

General Administration
(*a*) Effects of Government action.
(*b*) Legal and contractual obligations.

(*c*) Employee relations—including salary scales and conditions of employment.

(*d*) Dividend policy.

The five main problem areas and their sub-divisions include most of the cases where market information may be required. Clearly some of the problems will be of a continuous nature— e.g. inventory control, and some will occur infrequently—e.g. acquisition study or major investment appraisal. Hence the system must be capable of supplying continuous information for the continuous decisions and discrete quantities, if required, for the occasional decision. In addition it must use both internal and external sources.

Internal Sources

These are as follows

1. Statistical records such as tenders, orders, sales and deliveries by value, type of product and quantity.
2. Financial information—costs, profits, cash flows.
3. Product characteristics such as quality, attributes, weaknesses.
4. Research and development objectives and achievements.
5. Expert market knowledge of the marketing and sales personnel.
6. Others—such as administrative or professional experience.

External Sources

1. Published statistics.
2. Trade journals, catalogues and directories.
3. Trade, research and professional institutes and associations.
4. Government organisations such as the E.D.C.
5. Newspapers.
6. Contacts with competitors.
7. Feedback from customers.
8. Contacts with non-competitive companies who supply the same market.
9. Libraries.
10. Market surveys.

The vital question is how to set up an information system. A company can almost guarantee its success if it has available better information than its rivals and if it uses this information in an optimal manner. Hence the approach to building a formal system may be as follows

Specify the information needs of the organisation according to the criteria already discussed.

Examine the existing internal information structure to find out how it meets the requirements of the organisation.

Ensure that the internal statistics are in a usable form and are generated with sufficient speed and flow to the point of analysis.

Examine the existing flow from external sources to determine whether full use is being made of the information available.

Ensure that sufficient skilled personnel are available to provide continuous flow to the point of analysis.

Ensure that the natural market contacts, such as salesmen, have the opportunity and incentive to feed back data.

Construct an occupation model of the organisation to depict either departments or individuals and their particular characteristics, with respect to information potential and needs.

Provide each individual with an incentive and opportunity to feed information into the stream.

Set up a central control point, called the central analysis point until now, through which all information passes.

These are only the organisational requirements for information handling, and no mention is made of the mechanical methods available. In a well controlled organisation, computerised methods can mean fast analysis and instantaneous transmission of the results simultaneously to several different places, if a central system is used with remote terminals. Further, with high speed print outs and visual or audio methods now available there will be no fear of information 'not arriving'. If the data transmission to a particular point is considerable and storage facilities are limited, the printed or visual output may be transferred directly to microfilm, which incidentally now has up-dating capabilities. Because of the dynamic nature of business no central control can be completely up-to-date with the changing problems. The sales manager who segments his market geographically is usually interested in geographic breakdowns, but changing geographic patterns of demand may prompt him to segment

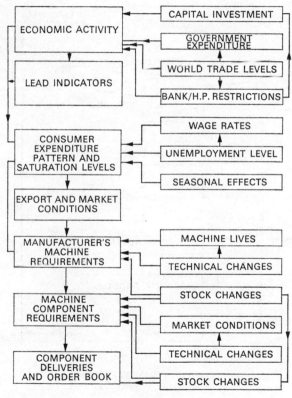

Figure 3

INFORMATION FRAMEWORK FOR
INDUSTRIAL MARKETING

according to some other criterion. Hence he needs to know the distribution of his total market by this new criterion. If the information is stored in the computer it is only necessary to call forward by this criterion.

The following diagrams illustrate some of the principal points made in this section. *Figure 3* gives the broad framework within which the marketing function is carried out. This shows some of the principal internal and external factors for which information may be required.

Figure 4 details in a general way how an information system might be formulated.

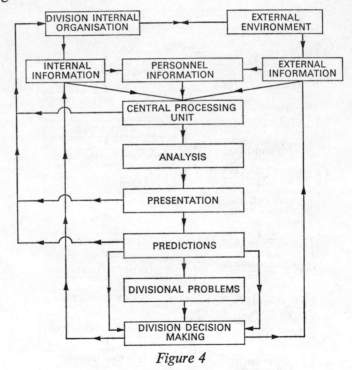

Figure 4

THE INFORMATION FLOW SYSTEM

HOW TO ASSESS THE WORTH OF ADDITIONAL INFORMATION AGAINST THE COST OF OBTAINING IT

For a given problem information gathering can often go on

indefinitely. Clearly there must be a point beyond which the marginal cost of collecting more information exceeds its worth. The value to the decision maker of further information at any given time, often follows a particular pattern. This general pattern takes the shape of the S-shaped curve otherwise known as the logistic (see *Figure 5*).

Figure 5 shows the cumulative value of information plotted against the cost of acquiring it. From the sketch it is seen that there is an initial period (A—B) which corresponds to the 'learning period'. This may simply be a period of familiarisation with the problem and its information requirements.

During the initial period A to B the value of information obtained is low relative to the cost because of the learning required. During period B—C a marginal increase in expenditure gives rise to a disproportionately high level of value.

The value obtained from each £1 spent increases to the point C when the rate of increase starts declining. From this point the value obtained per £1 spent decreases. The last stage eventually approaches the point when additional information is difficult or impossible to obtain. Alternatively it may

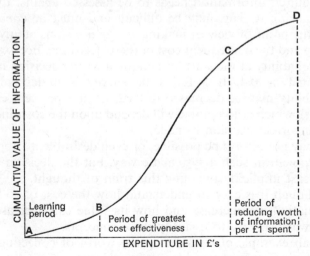

Figure 5

THE COST OF FURTHER INFORMATION AND ITS VALUE

correspond with the point where sufficient information had already been obtained for that specific problem.

If an attempt is to be made to estimate the likely time and cost involved then the first step is to consider the various ways in which the required information may be obtained. The various sources have already been mentioned and any combination of these may be applicable. If a company has a good information system, then the cost of locating internal information should be relatively small and readily calculable. If this is not the case, it can take considerable effort to locate the required data and it could be difficult to assess its cost.

In general it should be possible to estimate the cost of using external sources—for example, telephone calls, interviews, postal questionnaires, visual techniques, and literature searches. In the case of market surveys, certain parts lend themselves to quite precise costing, particularly if an outside agency is used and an exact price is quoted.

The major cost in gathering more information is the time it takes and the possible opportunity loss in delaying a decision. If these costs can be estimated approximately then the value of the required information needs to be assessed against the cost of acquiring it. This may be difficult and must be considered from the point of view of making wrong decisions at any point in time and the consequent cost of these decisions. For example, the probability at the start, of making a wrong decision may be estimated as 0·4. If a full scale survey is undertaken this probability may be decreased to 0·02, i.e. a 2 per cent chance. The risk which is acceptable will depend upon the costs incurred if an incorrect decision is made.

It may not always be possible, or even desirable, to approach the problem in such a systematic way, but the decision maker is at least implicitly pursuing this train of thought.

Although it is easy to understand how the cost of collecting information can increase and how its value can decrease, it is not always so easy to quantify these concepts.

As an example of considering the worth of collecting extra information a simple problem is considered.

Company X produces a component which is used in a wide variety of machinery. The number of manufacturers of the machinery is known. From previous surveys or published statistics the total population of machines can be calculated.

Since each machine uses one component and the component's life distribution is known, the total market for the component can be calculated.

Market intelligence reports that a major competitor is undertaking research and development with the aim of producing a modified component.

It is not known whether the competitor will be successful in the development, nor is it known for certain whether it will have sufficiently desirable features to adversely affect X's market share.

The problem is to assess the possible affects of this potential market threat and measure the consequent financial implications. On closer consideration it may seem more logical that the problem is really for Company X to decide whether or not to undertake Research and Development. There could also be other possibilities such as considering licence agreements.

If it is accepted that the real problem is to decide whether to undertake R. & D. or not, then assessing the effects of the threat and estimating the financial implications become forecasting requirements. Hence to forecast more accurately, better information is required—for example a survey to find out what customers think of the modification.

One solution is to rely on expert judgement to assess the probability of the competitor succeeding and to evaluate the likely effect on market share. This means estimating the cost to Company X if their competitor succeeds or fails, for both the cases where Company X undertakes or does not undertake research. Similarly the gains, if any, will have to be estimated.

The decision alternatives may be represented diagrammatically as shown in *Figure 6*. Although this decision tree shows only three different outcomes, in reality there could be many more. Further there may be opportunities for sequential decision making beyond that shown.

Figure 6 also shows that there are costs associated with the various acts that may be made (i.e. C_1, C_2) and that each event has a probability of occurring (P_1, P_2). Each branch eventually ends at some outcome which may be evaluated in financial

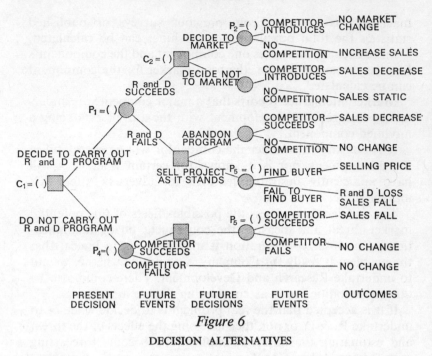

Figure 6

DECISION ALTERNATIVES

terms. This illustration is to demonstrate the value of the decision tree technique in displaying the decision logically and no real attempt is made to show how the best alternative may be selected.

It is clear that the information aspects of the problem may realistically be split into two parts

Estimation of the probability that market share will fall by a specified amount, given that the modification is successful, and,

estimation of the competitor's probability of success.

The order is reversed because the first point is the important one. This is in the sense that, if the modification is not considered advantageous by the potential customer, it does not matter if the competitor is certain of success. By the same token if its effect could be disastrous to the company then even a very low probability of success must be considered carefully.

If expert judgement suggested that the competitor had a 50 per cent chance of success and that the modification could cause a reduction of trading profit by 10 per cent, say £1m. in absolute terms, then the expected loss is £½m. Suppose that expert judgement suggested that the R. & D. programme would cost £10,000 with an 80 per cent probability of success.

Then from the tree diagram this could result in a 10 per cent increase in market share with probability $0.8 \times 0.5 = 0.4$ or expected value £400,000 — R. & D. expenditure = £390,000.

Without evaluating the alternatives in *Figure 6* it is obvious that with risks so high it is worthwhile attempting to estimate the various probabilities with greater precision. One way is to carry out a market survey in which respondents state whether they will switch to the modified component or not. This is naturally an over-simplification of the usual position but is sufficient to demonstrate the point. Suppose that there are 1,000 customers and that it costs £10 to get this information from each. Then 'certain' knowledge would cost £10,000.

If it were thought that 90 per cent would in fact change to the modified component then a sample could be taken to estimate the decline in market share with calculable probability. It would be possible to place a very high probability on this estimate. The sample size can be determined by standard statistical sampling methods and the total cost may be determined from a consideration of the variable and fixed costs— that is carrying out a survey may be judged at £X per week or month plus the number of interviews times the average interview cost.

If the survey result suggested that even if the modification were successful, it would have only very minor impact on the market, then the decision may very well be not to undertake R. & D.

If it is suggested that successful development could have serious effects then the next step is to attempt to gauge the probability that the competitor will succeed. Ways of doing this may include employing specialists to examine the technical requirements. Alternatively a realistic view of the probability of successful development may sometimes be obtained by looking at U.S. or European experience.

Neither the data nor the details in this example were meant to be any more than illustrative. Also there are very often a considerable number of options available to the company that identifies the threat in time. For example a licensing agreement may be obtained or product improvement combated by providing better service, lower prices or harder selling. If the new product really could be disastrous then even acquiring the competitor could be a possible alternative.

In later chapters, more detailed discussion will be given on assessing the value of further information by using Bayesian methods to adjust probabilities estimated on the basis of prior information.

UTILISING MARKET FEEDBACK

Taking as an example, the information which a salesman can collect and feed back, there are a number of ways this can be used. The necessary information flows must be set up and this may include the design or adaptation of appropriate forms as well as deciding upon the route they should take. In addition it may be necessary to brief the salesmen as to the sort of information which will be of greatest importance and ensure that there is real incentive to motivate them to collect it and pass it on. If it can be shown that the salesman will benefit directly from the system, then this should be sufficient incentive. It is important that proper controls are implemented to guard against biased information.

Having taken steps to ensure that the required information will be gathered and passed on, it is necessary that

facilities for proper analysis and interpretation are available; and

a mechanism is set up for feeding the results and recommendations, both to the decision points and also back to the data gatherers, where applicable.

For analysis and interpretation it is essential that at least one person is permanently involved in the information affairs of a specific part of the organisation. It may be that just one person is sufficient for a small operating group and that he should become a specialist in the affairs of the group. Feedback from salesmen would constitute only part of the total information flow. In addition the specialist must scan all relevant publications, make and keep contact with trade associations and industry. He will need to be able to assimilate technical data and decide upon the importance or relevance of company information, technological data, production methods and market information.

The information specialist must therefore know the problems facing the group and he must possess the appropriate analytical tools necessary for processing, analysing and re-distributing the information. He should also have sufficient authority to contact

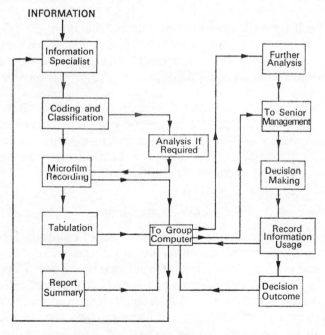

Figure 7

OUTLINE OF THE OVERALL INFORMATION FLOW SYSTEM

any member of the organisation and have access to confidential information.

It is essential that the external flow system functions in conjunction with the internal procedure and provides 'available' information and its analysis for senior management for use in decision making.

The specialist will be required to scan all relevant publications and extract the appropriate information. He should sort, classify and tabulate information in a continuous way, submitting regular reports to the appropriate decision points.

Such reports will probably be printed in the normal way whereas the basic information may be microfilmed.

The scanning and extracting operation must be based on a pre-determined coding so that each reference may be appropriately classified. It may then be microfilmed and fed directly into a computer where it is allocated to its appropriate file, identified by the code.

By coding and microfilming direct, the complete printed article is recorded and hence bias and misinterpretation are avoided. However the information arises, the source documents can be coded and microfilmed hence saving considerable time.

Figure 7 depicts an overall system. This in fact shows the computer as being central to the flow system. However, if a company is not sufficiently advanced in its communications to have computerised systems then the function may be taken on by a central management service department.

THE ROLE OF MARKET RESEARCH TECHNIQUES

Market research may be regarded as a set of methods designed to collect market information, analyse it and make inferences from the analysis. This defines what market research involves but the real purpose of market research is the application of this specific information and inferences to specific problems. In other words, the techniques of market research are used as tools in the decision making process.

The marketing manager who commissions a market research team to research his markets may respond to pertinent questions by saying that he particularly wants to find out the total market for a specific product. If he is questioned more deeply, he may reveal that he really wants to optimise his market budget allocation by sales area. He can therefore write down his problem in a systematic decision-alternative manner. He can consider allocating his total budget in a specific way on the assumption that the demand follows roughly the same proportion. He can postulate how he would expect demand to vary from area to area and indicate special reasons why there should be anomalies—for example a major competitor may get nearly all the local business in one area.

Once the alternatives are specified then, by asking him how likely the 'events' may be that he says may occur, it might be possible to calculate the cost of making the wrong decision on prior information only and thus the risk of loss. From such a representation it should be possible to decide not only how much information is required but also how much it may be worth. In addition it should be possible to tailor the survey design to meet these requirements in the most economic and speedy way.

Problem Areas Where Market Research Skills May be Relevant

The skills required in market research relate to the gathering, compiling, classifying and tabulating of information, and its proper analysis and interpretation. The problem areas which may be dealt with can range from analysis of economic trends, to short- and long-term environmental studies which may involve economic, political or social considerations.

If market research personnel are experienced in forecasting and using estimation methods they may happily take on the evaluation of sales and competitive trends. This may include studies of demand potential and evaluating optimal strategies for marketing budgets and salesmen allocation.

Studies may be made to find the effectiveness of packaging or advertising, to find new markets for old products or to assess the market prospects for a new product.

Another area of activity may be evaluating pricing policies and assessing the likely profitability of products under varying assumptions relating to design and marketing effort. Implicit or explicit in most analyses are demand studies and such studies may in turn require studies into consumer income and expenditure, industrial investment patterns and many other areas.

If the company is extensively involved in advertising, studies may arise to assess brand preferences, buying habits, advertising themes and use of the media. Assessing the effectiveness of advertising may be troublesome but investigation will often be beneficial.

Since a great deal of market research is often carried out without proper thought and consideration of the sampling and analytical tools which are available and applicable a number of these methods are briefly mentioned in the following pages. The aim is to provide a summary of methodology so that inexperienced researchers at least appreciate the range of methods available. There are only too many examples of expensive and well-intentioned surveys which have provided interesting but practically unusable results because of the lack of understanding of the basic principles involved in sample design. The biggest danger is that the researcher is totally unaware of research requirements, and therefore fails to safeguard his survey from this failure.

The first requirement in the selection of a sample, if proper inferences are to be drawn about the population, is that the sample units are selected randomly from the whole population. A random sample is one in which every unit in the population has an equal chance of being selected.

It is not selecting units in a haphazard manner as is often thought. This often results in an unrepresentative sample, and at worst is biased by the sampler. Take for example the case where salesmen are instructed to determine the market for a product they sell. They will almost inevitably produce a sample heavily biased towards their company's customers and this may be totally unrepresentative.

In industrial sampling it is often difficult to precisely specify the population and therefore randomness is seldom achievable to the extent that may be obtained in consumer research.

Another form of non-random sampling is often called

'purposive' sampling where the sample units are chosen by expert judgement. Unless the expert happens to be a real expert in that market, and a statistician, it is unlikely that sound statistical inference can be made.

In 'probability sampling' every member of the population has a known non-zero probability of being selected by using random methods. A sample design may be based on each member having the same probability or where different elements have different probabilities. Many well used designs are based on the last case and provide efficient methods.

A form of sampling which is often random is 'systematic' sampling where units are selected at a given interval, for example every twentieth on a list. There are of course some risks involved. One in particular is that the interval may possibly correspond with a regular attribute in the population.

One other form of selection procedure which may be rarely used is that of the 'capture/recapture' technique which has evolved for dealing with mobile populations.

Sample Designs

The sampling precision required will depend upon the problem being tackled and the sample size will depend upon the precision. This w ll be estimated from knowledge of the variable in the population being measured—that is its approximate distribution.

Stratified[1] sampling utilises knowledge about the population which permits its division into a number of homogeneous parts. Proportionate stratified sampling is where the sub-sample from each part or strata is chosen on a proportionate basis. Disproportionate stratified sampling is where the within-strata variance is taken into account. This procedure, by eliminating variance between strata, can produce much more precise information from a given sample size.

In cluster[2] sampling, the sample units are clusters of elements.

---

[1] Stratified sampling occurs when separate selections are made from partitions or strata of the population.
[2] Cluster sampling occurs when sample units are clusters of elements.

The clusters may be of equal or unequal size and one or more stages may be used.

Another useful method of sampling is two-phase sampling where the final sample is selected from a first-phase which obtains information for estimation or stratification. The relevance of this method to industrial research is where the population is ill-defined and the first-phase can often be used to specify it quickly.

Quota[1] sampling is another stratified method where the strata are constructed along the lines of those characteristics which are thought most to influence the variables being studied. A disadvantage of this method may be that the interviewer selects the sample units and therefore introduces bias.

Analytical Techniques

Multiple Regression and Correlation   Regression[2] analysis is a method of mathematically specifying a casual relationship between one variable, known as the dependent variable,[3] and one or more other variables, known as the independent variables.[4] Correlation[5] analysis attempts to measure association between two or more variables without attempting to specify a causal relationship. There is a vast body of methods available under this heading to deal with many different situations.

[1] Quota sampling is a form of purposive sampling where the interviewers are instructed to obtain given numbers within each of the relevant population strata.

[2] Regression is defined in the case of two variables by Thorton C. Fry in *Probability and its Engineering Uses* as follows: In the distribution p(x,y) for two chance variables x and y, the curve of regression of y on x is the locus of the conditional expectations $E_1(y/x)$. It is defined by the equation $y = E_1(y/x)$.

[3] Dependent variable is one whose values or levels are required to be explained or predicted.

[4] Independent variables are those whose values or levels are not required to be explained or predicted, and are either known in advance or can be considered to be fixed.

[5] Correlation analysis is a method for measuring the association between two or more variables where zero corresponds with 'no relationship' and unity corresponds with an exact relationship.

Multivariate Analysis These are statistical methods of describing and measuring interrelationships between sets of variables and reducing the number of variables to manageable proportions. Factor analysis for example, as with correlation analysis, is concerned with measuring association with no single variate considered at the start as being of greatest interest. The technique is used to identify basic factors which for example underlie consumers' preference for one brand over another. Other methods of dealing with multivariate problems include principal components analysis,[1] discriminating analysis,[2] canonical analysis,[3] latent structure analysis,[4] analysis of variance and co-variance.[5]

[1] Principal component analysis is concerned with evaluating underlying factors which influence some variable of interest.
[2] Discriminant analysis is similar to regression analysis except that it deals with dichotomous estimates (two category responses) in the dependent variable.
[3] Canonical analysis is often used to relate two or more behavioural characteristics with several socio-psychological variables.
[4] Latent structure analysis deals with dichotomous data.
[5] Analysis of variance and co-variance are methods of explaining variation in data and as a basis of experimental design.

Check List

1. Have you identified by name and briefed the members of the organisation charged with the:

(a) collection of information?

(b) distribution of information?

2. When information is stored is there a record of how it was used in a previous specific case and the outcome of using it?

3. Is an assessment made of the value of the information stored, i.e., its worth to the company against the cost of obtaining it?

4. Is the information system designed to provide strategic information to cover alternative courses of action?

5. Is the information system deliberately adapted to give quantitative answers?

6. After information has been used and a course of action taken, is the result examined to identify inaccuracies which have subsequently come to light?

7. Have the company's objectives been examined in the light of problems they are likely to encounter?

8. Have these problems been listed?

9. Has the company information system been designed primarily with these problems and the probability of their arising in mind?

10. Have the problems been divided formally, e.g., as

(a) production problems?

(b) sales problems?

(c) advertising problems?
(d) financial problems?
(e) general administration problems?

11. Have the sources of information been listed?
(a) internal sources?
(b) external sources?

12. Have the internal sources been examined to discover how far they have been designed to meet the requirements of the organisation?

13. Are the internal statistics in usable form?

14. Are they being produced sufficiently quickly?

15. Are they accurately directed to the point of analysis?

16. Is full use being made of them?

17. Has an occupation model been made of the organisation showing departments or individuals and their particular capacity to provide information?

18. Has an occupation model of the organisation been constructed to depict either the particular needs and characteristics of information for departments or individuals?

19. Are there incentives for each individual to feed information into the stream?

20. Do the instructions and questions to the information centre state precisely what facts and opinions are required and any time deadlines?

21. Is there a central analysis point through which all information passes? Has the cost of obtaining information been examined in terms of:
(a) the time taken?
(b) the cost of information from external sources ranging from telephone calls to the use of an outside research agency?
(c) the probable cost of wrong decisions taken on less information against the cost of delaying decisions with fuller information?

22. Is full use being made of information from:
    (*a*) overseas (particularly U.S. or European)?
    (*b*) market feedback; salesmen; trade association; the industry?

23. Are specialist reports being regularly prepared and submitted to the appropriate decision points?

24. Is the basic information being economically stored, e.g., microfilmed and coded?

25. If an outside market research agency is being used has it been properly briefed on:
    (*a*) precise nature of the problem?
    (*b*) the total information required?
    (*c*) the information already available for the outside agency from inside the company?

REFERENCES

'Fast access information retrieval', A. G. A. Pickford, *Aslib Proceedings*, Vol. 19, No. 3, March 1967

Survey Sampling, L. Kish, Wiley, New York, 1965

Marketing and Market Assessment, J. L. Sewell, Routledge & Kegan Paul Limited, 1966

Sampling Techniques, W. G. Cochran, New York, Wiley, 1963

Sample Design in Business Research, W. G. Denning, New York, Wiley, 1960

The Foundation of Statistics, L. J. Savage, New York, Wiley, 1954

The Foundations of Statistical Inference, L. J. Savage, London, Methuen & Co., 1957

Introduction to Statistics for Business Decisions, R. Schlaifer, New York, McGraw-Hill, 1961

Sampling Methods for Censuses and Surveys, F. Yates, London, Chas. Griffin & Company, 1960

Methods of Correlation and Regression Analysis, M. Ezekial and K. A. Fox, New York, Wiley, 1959

Factor Analysis in Market Research, A. S. C. Ehrenberg, B.M.R.B. Limited Research Paper No. 1, 1959

'Application of co-variance analysis to marketing problems',
   P. L. Henderson, Proceedings of 124th Meeting of American
   Statistical Association, 1964
'Canonical analysis: An exposition and illustrative example',
   P. Green *et al.*, *Journal, Marketing Research*, 3
'Multivariate analysis for marketing research: an evaluation',
   Ronald Gatty, *Journal of The Royal Statistical Society*,
   Vol. XV, No. 3, 1966

CHAPTER 3

Some Forecasting Methodology in Marketing

Before examining in detail the role that expert judgement plays in decision making it is necessary to specify the main stages in a problem. These were mentioned in the introduction and are specified here for easy reference throughout the book.

The problem arises

The problem is clarified and an understanding and identification of its principle parts and characteristics is obtained.

From the clear formulation of the problem an information need is generated.

A preliminary analysis is made of the information readily available.

The statement of all the realistic different decision alternatives available is prepared.

The different events which may occur are listed.

The collection of as much further information as possible, within the time and cost constraints that exist is conducted.

An analysis is made of this information to assess the probabilities with which different states may occur and the affect of these occurrences given that a specific decision alternative is selected.

If further information is obtainable at extra cost or time, its worth is evaluated.

The most favourable alternative in terms of expected pay-offs is selected.

The risks involved in making this specific decision are assessed.

The alternative chosen is considered in terms of company policies and objectives.

The chosen alternative is implemented.

A feedback mechanism is set up to examine the actual outcome.

An evaluation of the final outcome, favourable or not, is carried out in retrospect, to learn from both successes and failures.

These stages are not necessarily in a fixed order nor are they mutually exclusive. In most, some measure of expert judgement is required and it is likely that such judgement, to some extent, always will be required. Even if perfect information were available and it was known that a particular event was certain to occur, it is possible that its effects on the alternative chosen were not considered to be important.

The three essential attributes which the successful decision maker must possess are experience, knowledge of appropriate techniques of analysis and expert judgement. The latter is often a function of the first and sometimes of the first and second combined. This means that a decision maker with considerable experience will often be able to choose the right alternative by judgement. If he understands the principles of probability and analysis it is likely that his judgement will be good even if his experience is relatively short.

Expert judgement is typically required as follows

In estimating the severity of the problem and deciding upon its relevance and importance to the organisation.

In assessing the extent of the information requirements, interpreting analytical results and especially in the formulation of appropriate hypotheses.

In deciding upon realistic alternatives and avoiding serious omissions.

In deciding upon which of the possible events are either most likely or most relevant and avoiding serious omissions.

In setting priorities and deciding when to stop searching for information and in the allocation of costs and time.

In interpreting the results of the analyses and in assessing risk.

In evaluating the worth of further data.

In making subjective probability estimates.

In assessing the compatability of the chosen decision alternative with overall objectives.

In choosing the right approach in implementation and especially in assessing the personalities involved.

The prediction process is applicable to all stages in that probability estimates, implicit or explicit, are made in each case. This implies that mathematical techniques are associated with subjective judgement methods in attempting to use all the available information. In addition, hypotheses and conclusions, need to be subjected to testability[1] by both subjective and empirical[2] methods.

So far, the role of expert judgement has been considered within the overall framework of decision making. This is necessary to appreciate its use in forecasting. It cannot, of course, be over-emphasised how important judgement is to the predictive process because of inadequate information or inadequate techniques. Hence the complete forecasting system will always include a subjective component—that is an area of application where expert judgement is required. Before considering forecasting models based on judgement alone it is

[1] Testability means open to independent and objective critical examination.
[2] Empirical means based on historical data.

necessary to define the complete system. This definition is in terms of its characteristics.

Firstly the system must be formulated on the basis of the criteria imposed by the specific problems with which it deals. The system may be set up to deal with one specific problem, say inventory control, or to deal with a set of problems. In the latter case it may not be practicable to build a model which adequately deals with each problem and some compromise must be sought. It is probably undesirable to have a very accurate system, if accuracy is equivalent to cost, when such accuracy is rarely required and the usual requirement is relatively low precision.

Secondly, the complete system should be a logical representation as far as possible of the prevailing situation. This representation need not be mathematical but obviously describing a system by equations permits rigorous analysis.

Thirdly, it should respond quickly to significant changes in, say, demand but slowly to random fluctuations. If it is sensitive to changes due to assignable causes, it will also be sensitive to random fluctuations, and therefore a compromise must be sought.

The fourth characteristic is that it should be part of a control system. This has been discussed in detail in chapter 2. In addition to being part of an overall control system it should have its own tracking system. This would preferably be mathematically based with the opportunity for subjective testability.

The fifth characteristic is that the time taken and cost of producing a prediction must be compatible with the problems being tackled. The efficiency of the model should be estimable. For example, the cost of building and maintaining it must be compared with those of alternative methods, in terms of its predicting accuracy and the cost involved. It must be able to specify the probability distribution of some future estimate.

The sixth characteristic which should be sought is simplicity, but not to the exclusion of other properties. Certainly the simpler it is to understand the better the chance of it being used properly.

The seventh characteristic is that the system should use all available information—within the normal cost and time considerations. Every effort should be made to quantify whatever relationships are used.

It cannot be over-emphasised that the preceding properties are those which should be sought under ideal conditions. Naturally, in the business situation where both time and cost constraints apply it may not be possible for the model to have all these attributes.

THE ROLE OF SALESMEN'S FORECASTS

Estimates of, say, future demand or the probability of getting a particular order may be made by personnel in close contact with the market. Salesmen are of course in the position to make such estimates and therefore it is pertinent to consider their role in the forecasting system.

For reference, a system which uses only such subjective estimates is termed a 'purely subjective model'. In such a model there are obvious dangers—for example, salesmen may tend to be over-optimistic when quoting the probability of getting an order. Further, it is unlikely that long-term forecasts will be very reliable.

While there are very real dangers in relying exclusively on a 'purely subjective' model, personnel in specific market functions often have access to considerable information which may never be objectively processed. Hence their estimates will be determined even if in an unsystematic way by their specific knowledge. If a proper information system is used (i.e. as in chapter 1), then risks of bias or omission can be minimised and the information from salesmen can be judged against that from other sources. Where such information systems do not exist some use can still be made of the estimates. One way is by attempting to measure the effectiveness of the salesmen as forecasters by comparing their estimates with what actually happens. If a particular salesman consistently forecasts demand above that which occurs, careful questioning may reveal the reason. Once this is understood, it may be possible to decrease the bias.

Another approach may be to get salesmen to specify the numerical probabilities that they attach to the success of each order or different demand levels. By a combination of explanation and careful questioning useful results may be obtained.

Another method is to use expert judgement in conjunction with an objective mathematical model. This ceases to be a 'purely subjective' model since it now contains an objective element.

It is most important that in striving towards objectivity, field information is not neglected or relegated to an unimportant position. After all, one of the purposes of building a forecasting model is to simulate the actual business situation and what successful entrepreneurs already do. If such simulation is on a consistent and systematic basis using all relevant and validated available information there are advantages. The most important advantage is that the formal model can be examined and tested and if errors occur, causes can be determined. Hence forecasting ability improves.

Again, there are too few successful entrepreneurs to go around and if a company does have one there are inherent risks in relying on him too much, rather than constructing sound systems. Success may be due to a large slice of good luck and good luck has a habit of running out from time to time.

USES AND LIMITATIONS OF TIME SERIES ANALYSIS

A time series is an ordered sequence of events such as a company's sales recorded monthly. Analysis of time series is carried out to determine patterns or characteristics which may either repeat themselves or persist into the near future.

There are two reasons why time series analysis may be useful —one is as an aid to understanding how the organisation works, that is attempting to represent historical occurrences. The second reason is to use such a presentation, modified if necessary, to predict future events.

Ideally, time series analysis should be a first step towards building a more sophisticated model depicting, say, changes in demand level related to various economic, industrial or socio-logical factors. In the time series model these causative factors are implicitly replaced by one independent variable, time. The model may not therefore indicate the reasons why change occurs, but under certain circumstances may yield good estimates of future demand.

The reasoning behind the use of this type of model is that if a series has exhibited particular characteristics in the past then it is likely to continue to do so in the future. This is logical only if the underlying factors that influence it are known, and if it is thought that these factors will continue to behave in the same way as they behaved during the period under investigation. The extent to which the underlying factors may change in behaviour determines the extent to which extrapola-tion[1] may be carried out and the degree of confidence[2] that may be placed on the estimates. It is often argued that the longer the series, or the more consistent it is, the more trust that can be put on the estimates obtained by extrapolation. This assertion is intuitively appealing but not beyond doubt.

The fact remains that time series analysis can yield quick and good results, especially when used for short-term forecasting. Hence these techniques may be valuable but usage should be restricted to the following circumstances:

When short-term forecasting only is required and in conjunc-tion with a built-in safety valve that automatically signals when an observation is recorded which is significantly different from the forecast level. This difference will usually be measured in purely statistical terms and be based on the standard error[3] of estimate, which is a measure of how closely the model represented the data in the past.

[1] Extrapolation means projecting a relationship beyond the range of the historical data.
[2] Degree of confidence relates to the amount of variation thought to be applicable around the point estimate.

[3] The standard error of estimate is a mathematical measure of the amount of variation which exists round the point estimate. This may be expressed as a range of values within which the population parameter is expected to lie.

As a preliminary investigation or basis to more sophisticated model.

If quick decisions are required for either mid- or long-term planning when it is preferable to rapidly analyse the historical data rather than guess.

When no economic or sociological data is available and hence more sophisticated models are not possible.

Whenever forecasts are made, based on time series analysis, whatever expert knowledge is available should be used. Some caution in extrapolating must be observed however well the equation fits the historical data. There are classical cases where predictions based on second order or higher order polynomials[1] were incorrect.

TIME SERIES ANALYSIS METHODOLOGY

General Approach

The first step in time series analysis is to obtain a series which is suitable for analysis. This may seem obvious but the series of data must be examined for reliability, consistency, completeness, and changes in definition. Every effort must be made to ensure that each value has been recorded on the same basis and that no available or relevant information has been excluded. For example, in using sales data it is easy to produce underestimates by omitting unfulfilled orders. If the basic data is unreliable then the results may also be unreliable and statements of probabilities may not be possible.

All this is obvious enough but when it is remembered that the historical data is the foundation of the forecasting model it will be realised just how important it is to spend some time in checking.

Having ascertained that the data is satisfactory, or the best available, a convenient starting point is to plot the series on arithmetic or logarithmic graph paper. It is often easier to

[1] A polynomial is an equation which has terms raised to powers such as x^2, $x^3 \ldots x^n$.

5

discern trends or cyclic changes from such a visual representation than by looking at the series itself. Also, by intelligent use of visual methods and using appropriate data transformations,[1] for example plotting the logarithms or reciprocals of the values, the time spent in analysis can often be reduced.

The next step is to examine the plotted data for violent fluctuations or inconsistencies. If any exist, it is often worthwhile attempting to establish the causes. This would be with the view to determining whether these events are likely to recur in the prediction period.

There are several methods of analysis and these are considered under the heading of the various models that may be used.

Model 1: Arithmetic Moving Averages

The simplest model is the additive system where the time series is considered to consist of several additive components such as trend, seasonal or cyclic parts. 'Additive' means that the sum of the components equals the estimate at a given point in time.

The trend is the overall direction in which the series moves and it may be obscured in the basic data by a combination of random fluctuations,[2] cyclic, and seasonal changes. If instead of plotting the basic data, averages of several periods are plotted, the nature of the trend may be seen. In other words a smoothing operator is used—this being the moving average. Obviously if the series consists of monthly data then using a moving average based on twelve observations should smooth out the seasonal component. For if the smoothed values are subtracted from the actual observations, the differences are likely to be cyclical over each twelve-month period, that is the seasonal component. In addition there may be a large cycle every four or five years and this may be the economic cyclic affect.

If there is an obvious seasonal component then this can be

---

[1] A data transformation is expressing the basic data in terms of some function of it—for example if the series is x_i then this may be transformed to log x_i by taking the logarithm of each value of the series.

[2] Random fluctuations are variations due to unassigned causes.

determined by averaging the differences for a particular month over several years. For example, toy sales will generally have a seasonal peak about December. If the moving average for December is deducted from the observed value for that month, for each of several years, then the average of these differences will be the seasonal component and this may itself be changing.

When the seasonal effects have been estimated for each month or period, these may be removed from the model by subtraction from the actual sales values for each corresponding month or period. The data is now said to be deseasonalised and if it is plotted out will show less fluctuation than the basic data.

Cyclic affects may be calculated in a similar way and subtracted from the deseasonalised data, to leave the basic trend and random fluctuations. If a line is drawn through the data adjusted for seasonal and cyclic affects, the data will lie above and below the line—only a few points are likely to lie on it. The differences between the trend lines and the plot-points represent fluctuations due to unassigned causes and are termed residual variations. The line which is drawn through the data may be estimated by eye, fitted by mathematical methods described later, or by averaging.

When the residuals have been calculated these may be examined to determine whether their magnitude or direction is influenced by external factors such as economic changes, occurrence of holidays or special events, meteorological conditions or many other factors. There are statistical methods available for carrying out such examinations—for example to test whether successive residuals are independent or not.

Having fitted an appropriate curve an extrapolation is made to the point for which a forecast is required and this trend value is taken as the forecast trend at that point. The seasonal affect and cyclic effects corresponding with this month or period are added to or deducted from this trend value. In addition any information about the possible occurrence of events which could affect the forecast should be recorded.

The final stage once the forecasting system is functioning properly is to put it on to a systematic basis so that as new data becomes available the forecasts are checked and the latest information is incorporated into the model. Again statistical methods, such as cumulative sum techniques,[1] are available for deciding whether a system is going out of control or not.

It is obvious that the linear moving average method is not totally satisfactory since the moving average based on averaging twelve-month periods for instance is representative of a point six periods in the past. Hence full account is not taken of the last six observations. Also, as the number of periods in the average increases, the system becomes decreasingly sensitive to significant change.

The main applications of this model are:

Short-term forecasting of consumer goods, in particular where demand is changing at a very steady rate.

Smoothing data graphically, which sometimes permits a better estimate of trend to be made where the data is very irregular.

As a preliminary exercise before further investigation.

The main advantages of using a moving average method is that it is fast, cheap and very easy to understand. In addition it is easy to operate, and several computer programmes are available to simplify its implementation even further. Providing the number of periods in the average is chosen with reasonable care irregularities in the data may be smoothed with not too great a loss of sensitivity.

The chief disadvantages are that the latest data is not fully used and hence the average will often respond too slowly to significant change. The simple mathematical treatment of this model is in reference 1 of the appendix.

As an example of using arithmetic moving averages the data shown below represents demand for certain optical instruments over thirteen periods. Demand is to the nearest £25,000 and the overall trend over the thirteen periods appears to be linear with a cyclic variation around the trend having a periodicity of four to five periods.

---

[1] Cumulative sum techniques are methods for monitoring and control of actual results against those forecast.

Period	Demand in £000	Moving Total	Four-year Moving Total	Four-year Moving Average	Centred Average
1	125	125			
2	200	325		175	
3	200	525		194	185
4	175	700	700	200	197
5	200	900	775	225	213
6	225	1,125	800	281	253
7	300	1,425	900	338	310
8	400	1,825	1,125	381	360
9	425	2,250	1,350	400	390
10	400	2,650	1,525	406	403
11	375	3,025	1,600	419	413
12	425	3,450	1,625		
13	475	3,925	1,675		

The basic demand data is shown plotted in *Figure 8* which also shows a four-year moving average—that is the dotted line. Clearly the moving average smoothes through the basic data and indicates the overall trend.

The moving total in the table is obtained simply by summing up demand in successive periods. The four-year moving total is derived from the moving total at a specific period by subtracting the moving total in the fourth period before. For example, the four-year moving total applicable to period six is $1,125 - 325 = 800$. The four-year moving average is then obtained by dividing the four-year moving totals by 4. In order that the value so obtained can be related to specific periods and not to a time midway between two periods it is necessary to 'centre' the moving average. This is simply by adding two successive values of the moving average and dividing by 2. For example the un-centred moving average for the first four periods relates to a point between period two and period three. When this is centred, as explained the moving average for that period relates to period three.

To use the moving average for predicting, the trend—that is the dotted line in *Figure 8*—may be extended by eye to the point for which a forecast is required. If a regular cycle has been observed in the past data then an adjustment can be made for the position in the cycle of the predicted point. As an example, if peaks occur in the second, sixth and tenth periods, then a prediction for the fourteenth period would consist of a trend value plus an additional amount to allow for the position in the cycle. In the example shown in *Figure 8* there appears to be a cycle but it is difficult to estimate its periodicity from the data available. However the series increases from period four to period nine and on this limited information it may be assumed that it will also increase from period eleven to period sixteen. Naturally such assumptions would be subject to knowledge of possible changes in the underlying causative factors.

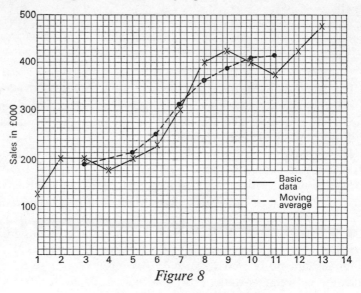

Figure 8

GRAPH SHOWING N-PERIOD MOVING AVERAGE

Model II: The Multiplicative Case

In this model it is assumed that the time series consists of several multiplicative components. Multiplicative means that when the components are multiplied together at a given point in time, the result is the estimate for that period. A typical case might be where the amplitude of the cycle is growing. The method of analysis is the same as for the Additive Case except that the components are removed by division. For instance the seasonal component may be represented by a proportion which is greater than one at the seasonal peak and less than one at the seasonal trough, and the data is divided by this proportion to remove the seasonal affect. The advantages and disadvantages of the Multiplative model are the same as for the Additive model. Mathematical representation is given in reference 2 of the appendix.

Model III: Exponentially-Smoothed Moving Averages

The exponentially-smoothed moving average model is similar to Model I except that greater weight is given to current observations. This removes the defect in that method of the last $n/2$ values not being fully used. It is intuitively appealing in the sense that if any previous period has any affect at all on a future one, it is more likely to be the current one. Hence the last observation in the series is given a greater weight and the moving average is based on these weighted values.

Suppose that sales for the twelve months to the end of June are known and it is required to make a prediction for July. The expected forecast is given by a weighted average of actual sales in June and the forecast for June which was made in May. Similarly the forecast for June is the weighted average of actual sales in May and the forecast for May made in April. The weights used in the model can be chosen by trial and error until the model is reasonably representative of the series. At the extreme, if the weighting factor is unity then each forecast is the same value as the actual sales in the preceding period.

Seasonal factors can be incorporated into the exponentially-smoothed model by expressing the seasonal affect in terms of components. These may be additive or multiplicative. In many cases seasonal variation is periodic, being wave-like so that adjacent months have seasonal factors which are more alike than those for months far apart. If the factor changes for one month then it is also likely to change for adjacent months. The harmonic representation may be made by using expressions which involve trigonometric functions—for example sines and cosines.

The exponentially-smoothed model has greatest applicability where reasonably long time series are available and especially where demand changes regularly. Again as in the case of the arithmetic moving average, it is often useful to smooth the data exponentially before proceeding with further analysis. If the values in one period are related to one in an earlier period, this type of model may be very useful.

The main advantages are similar to those of the arithmetic model in that the method is fast and cheap and relatively easy to understand. The method also smooths irregularities but has the greater advantage of utilising all the data giving greater weight to the most recent values. If the weights are properly chosen it can be made to respond rapidly to real change but slowly to random fluctuations. This model is described mathematically in the appendix, reference 3.

As a simple example of the way in which data may be exponentially smoothed, the series on page 69 is considered. A weighting factor is chosen—by trial and error—and the successive values in the series are multiplied by the factors derived from this weighting, to obtain an exponentially-smoothed moving average.

If the weighting factor is assumed to be 0·8 then the latest value in the series is multiplied by this, the preceding value in the series by $0·8 \times (1 - 0·8)$, and the value immediately before that by $0·8 \times (1 - 0·8)^2$. This process is continued until a particular period's contribution to the moving average is negligible.

In the appendix, reference 3, it is shown how the computation is simplified by relating the moving average for the current period to that for the period immediately before. In symbols this is—

$$M_t = M_{t-1} + a(Y_t - M_{t-1})$$

Where M_t is the value of the moving average for period t
and M_{t-1} is the value of the moving average for the previous period
and a is the weighting factor
and Y_t is the current observation.
Using the data shown on page 69 and denoting the periods one to thirteen so that the moving average for the last period is

M_{t13}, the calculations are as shown below. The first four averages are calculated by working out each weighting factor to illustrate the method; the remainder are calculated by using the simplified expression $M_t = M_{t-1} + a(Y_t - M_{t-1})$.

Series (Y_{ti})	Calculation of exponentially smoothed average	(M_{ti}) Value of Average
125	$M_{t1} = aY_{t1} = 0.8 \times 125 = 100$	100
200	$M_{t2} = aY_{t2} + a(1-a)\,Y_{t1} =$ $0.8 \times 200 + 0.16 \times 125 = 160 + 16$	176
200	$M_{t3} = aY_{t3} + a(1-a)\,Y_{t2} +$ $a(1-a)^2\,Y_{t1} = 0.8 \times 200 +$ $0.16 \times 200 + 0.032 \times 125$	181
175	$M_{t4} = 0.8 \times 175 + 0.16 \times 200 +$ $0.032 \times 200 + 0.0064 \times 125$	175
200	$M_{t5} = M_{t4} + 0.8\,(Y_{t5} - M_{t4}) =$ $175 + 0.8\,(200 - 175)$	195
225	$M_{t6} = M_{t5} + 0.8\,(Y_{t6} - M_{t5}) =$ $195 + 0.8\,(225 - 195)$	219
300	$M_{t7} = M_{t6} + 0.8\,(Y_{t7} - M_{t6})$	284
400	$M_{t8} = M_{t7} + 0.8\,(Y_{t8} - M_{t7})$	377
425	$M_{t9} = M_{t8} + 0.8\,(Y_{t9} - M_{t8})$	415
400	$M_{t10} = M_{t9} + 0.8\,(Y_{t10} - M_{t9})$	403
375	$M_{t11} = M_{t10} + 0.8\,(Y_{t11} - M_{t10})$	381
425	$M_{t12} = M_{t11} + 0.8\,(Y_{t12} - M_{t11})$	416
475	$M_{t13} = M_{t12} + 0.8\,(Y_{t13} - M_{t12})$	463

The basic data and smoothed moving average is shown plotted in *Figure 9* on page 74.

To use the model for forecasting the analyst may take the latest value of the moving average as the best estimate of the next period's demand. Another method which has frequently given reasonable results is to use the latest value but adjusted by the difference between that value and the previous period's moving average. In other words as an estimate of M_{t14}—that is the next period's value of the smoothed moving average—use

$$M_{t14} = M_{t13} + 0.8\,(M_{t13} - M_{t12})$$

In the numerical example given this yields

$$M_{t14} = 463 + 0.8\,(463 - 416) = 511.$$

This value is certainly consistent with both the general trend and the position of the fourteenth period on the apparent cycle. It may therefore be used as the 'one period ahead' forecast on the assumption that no underlying structural changes are occurring, and the further assumption that the forecaster has neither more time nor budget available to build a more comprehensive model.

Model IV: Adaptive Forecasting Model

The adaptive model is another exponential smoothing system based on weighted averages of two sources of evidence—the last observation and the previous period's calculated expected value. If the previous period was forecast too high then the forecast for the next period is adapted by this difference. A typical practical case is where higher than expected demand occurs in a particular month. It may then be argued that this was due to exceptional circumstances and that there will be some tendency towards trend. Hence the next forecast is modified downwards.

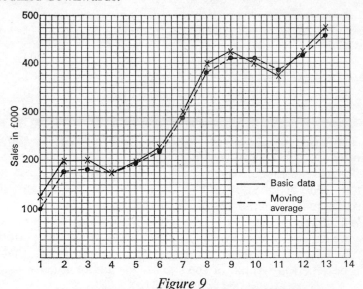

Figure 9

GRAPH SHOWING EXPONENTIALLY-SMOOTHED
MOVING AVERAGE

Trend Curves

The main assumption in using trend methods is that if a demand series has remained reasonably stable with respect to a particular function, in the past *n* periods, then it is likely to continue in a similar way in the future. Providing trend methods are used with caution—for example by ensuring that up-to-date information is available and is used to modify the forecasts—the methods are very useful especially where the forecaster has limited resources.

In the literature on forecasting the models already mentioned and their variants are sometimes described as trend curves. The division in this chapter is more for convenience in that the methods to be discussed are appropriate to both long- and short-term forecasting whereas Models I to IV find greatest application in short-term forecasting. *Figure 10* on page 76 demonstrates the main types of trend curves.

Model V: The Linear Model

If sales data are plotted on arithmetic graph paper and appear to form a scatter of points round a straight line, then a linear equation of the form shown in appendix reference 4, may be fitted to the data.

The linear model is applicable to a situation where demand is increasing or decreasing by a constant amount each period. The extent to which the plotted points lie on the straight line indicate the extent to which the line fits the data. For example if each point were actually on the line then this would be considered to be an excellent fit and the forecaster may have considerable confidence in using it to predict future sales.

Model VI: The Curvilinear Model

If demand is accelerating or decelerating the data, when plotted on arithmetic graph paper, may form a scatter around a curved line. A quadratic for example is an equation which has terms up to and including the power of 2 and is a line with a single curve, whereas a cubic equation—that is with terms up to and including the power of 3 will have two bends in it. In general an equation of the appropriate degree, called a polynomial, can be found to fit any curve.

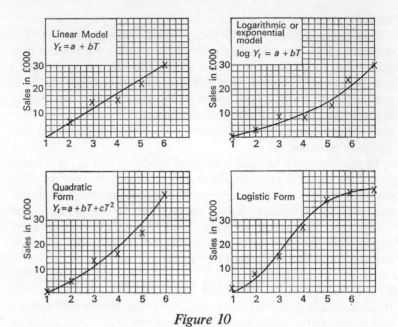

Figure 10

TREND CURVES (MODELS V, VI & VII)

In practice it is unusual to require for sales forecasting an equation with terms above the quadratic. Whenever non-linear equations are used very great care should be taken when projecting forward as there will be substantial danger in overestimating or underestimating in the long-term.

There are a number of non-linear equations which have terms involving logarithms that are very useful in describing specific situations. The exponential, modified exponential, Gompertz and logistic are grouped together under Model VII.

Model VII: Exponential Type Models

If demand for a product is increasing at an accelerating rate then the data when plotted on arithmetic graph paper will be scattered around a line which curves upwards. If the data is now plotted on semi-logarithmic paper, which is special graph paper in which the vertical scale is logarithmic rather than arithmetic, the plotted data may appear to be scattered around a straight line.

This would be in the case where demand is increasing by approximately a constant ratio—that is compound interest.

A straight line could then be drawn through the plotted points—or fitted mathematically—and this could be used for forecasting. Plotting the demand data on semi-log paper gives the same result as expressing each value in terms of logarithms and plotting on arithmetic graph paper. If for example the series of demand data is represented by Y where Y_i is the actual level of demand in period T_i then plotting the Y_i against the appropriate T_i on semi-log paper is the same as plotting log Y_i against T_i on arithmetic graph paper.

The concept used here is that of making a 'transformation' to examine the data more fully—in this case a logarithmic transformation. A straight line relationship between demand (Y_i) and time (T_i) is written

$$Y_i = a + bT_i$$

(where a and b are parameters corresponding respectively with the position of the line and its direction).

The exponential or logarithmic type relationship is written

$$\log Y_i = a + bT_i$$

The parameter a indicates the position of the line by indicating where the line cuts the vertical axis—that is where $T_i = 0$; the parameter b indicates the direction of the line as measured by the angle between the line and the horizontal axis.

In the appendix, reference 4, it is shown how the values of a and b may be mathematically estimated by the method of least squares.

There are many possible variations of this type of model—for example transformation of both variables or the independent variable alone. These transformations may be logarithmic, by taking reciprocals or other simple arithmetic changes, or by expressing in terms of trigonometric functions such as sines and cosines. The latter may be particularly suitable when for example the series exhibits a clear economic cycle.

A particularly useful equation in the family of exponential types is the logistic, which is used to describe phenomena such as the cumulative sales of a product over its life cycle and the penetration of a new market. This curve was mentioned on page 41 when it was used in *Figure 5* on page 41 to demonstrate how the cumulative worth of information varies with its value. The gently increasing initial part of the S-shaped curve corresponds with the introduction of say the new product and the learning period needed by the market. This is followed by a period of rapid penetration as the product becomes accepted and sought after by the market. The last period is where the market reaches saturation point, or competitive reaction occurs, and the rate of growth falls off. A simple method of fitting the logistic curve to data is described in appendix, reference 5; this is called the 'three-point method'.

The seven models and their variants are just a few examples of the very wide choice of models available in time series analysis. Whatever model is used, and however well it fits the data, the forecaster should never deceive himself that either mathematical complexity or closeness of fit guarantee the forecasts he makes. The forecaster should never forget the basic objective of trying to specify his forecasting problem in terms of logic, cause and affect, and explanation. He must always attempt to use all the information that he can readily obtain and set up systems so that the forecasts can always be revised in the light of additional information.

Summary of Time Series and Trend Forecasting Methodology

In the preceding sections the main emphasis has been on methods by which a prediction in a future period is based on times series analysis. To the exponential-smoothing models may be added such topics as Spectral Analysis—a field which is worth exploration.

It is important that a forecasting system should be set up on a systematic basis so that new data is automatically used to check and adjust it. Considerable research has been done on control methods such as cumulative sum or backward sequential methods and in the complete system some such method should be used. Apart from a mathematical control which signals when an observation is recorded which is larger than would be expected by random fluctuations there must also be a formal method for the flowback of expert market knowledge. This too must be analysed and adjustments made in the light of the latest information. A typical case is where a large deviation occurs but it is learnt that it is due to some extraordinary factor which has a very low probability of recurring. Another case is where it is known a month in advance that there will be a strike for a given period. Here, demand may very well remain at about the level predicted but output would have to be revised. Hence if demand is not met in that month there will be a carry over of demand in the following month. Alternatively, customers may order this month to avoid being disappointed next month and hence create an artificially high demand this month.

In the time series approach it is difficult to build into the model industrial or economic factors which influence demand. Since it is more logical to predict from a model which expresses the relationship between variables, the 'econometric' approach will be discussed in some detail in chapter 4.

THE INTERACTION OF EXPERT JUDGEMENT AND MATHEMATICALLY
DERIVED FORECASTS

A fully integrated model must be designed to use all available information in the best possible way. 'Best' in this sense does not imply that in a given situation a perfect operating model can be obtained. It really means the logical use of numerical data, its analysis and the logical use of non-numeric information.

The proper selection of the mathematical model should never be separated from available information, because knowledge of the system being represented is required in order to select the appropriate model. Such knowledge is also required to make adjustments to the model and to test it. Hence it will usually be unsatisfactory to develop a system based solely on historical data, although of course time and cost constraints may prevent a thorough study.

Broadly therefore, expert judgement, based on knowledge of the system, is required in order to decide which model is most likely to represent it. After such selection, expert judgements are required at virtually every point in its operation and its use.

The question is how to make the best use of expert judgement. There is no clear cut answer, because such judgement is based on a mixture of past experience of similar situations and knowledge of the current case. While there is no clear cut answer, there are certainly ways of increasing the probability of being right and also of improving judgement by experience.

The place to start is by ensuring that the organisation has a comprehensive information system. This ensures that judgements are at least based on all current knowledge. If such a system exists, the next step is to ensure that the personnel who need to make judgements are properly fitted into the system and hence obtain rapid access to the information they need. In addition personnel must be employed who have the right qualities and training to make good use of the information—for example, economists, statisticians, business analysts. The last essential ingredient is that the current problems must be properly understood, and also the factors affecting the organisation.

These are the ingredients—personnel, information and understanding—which are necessary for proper judgements to be made. Although it may not be possible to specify *precisely* how or why a particular statement is made, in most cases reasons can usually be given. If an estimate is made of the probability with which an event may occur then in general there are specific reasons why the particular value or range was chosen. If these reasons are stated explicitly then the probability statement may be examined for its 'reasonableness'. If such independent examination reveals no irrationality then it may be used. If it does not appear to be reasonable, then the originator of the estimate may be required to think again and revise his estimate. Of course, this does not 'ensure' success—it only decreases the risk of failure. With experience, however, it may very well be found that such risk often becomes negligible.

The ideas in this section are essentially based on the proposition that rational people, armed with the same information and familiar with the same analytical techniques, will tend to reach the same conclusion in given circumstances. In other words, the role of hunch is not accepted as being part of expert judgement. Certainly in most cases of, say, scientific discovery the 'strokes of genius' are usually the result of prolonged thought, hard work and full use of information.

There is, of course, one undeniably weak link in this proposition—simply that no two men can have precisely the same experience nor have they exactly similar personal data processing units (brains). Therefore, there may very well be cases where a particular judgement is made which is not accepted by the originator's colleagues. This is a formidable stumbling block but not insuperable. Adequate information, and proper use of decision analysis techniques must reduce such cases to a very low level, and when they do occur there are two possible approaches. The first is to decide on a democratic basis—that is a majority view. This may work in many cases, but it is just possible that major opportunities will be missed. The second approach is to accept the estimate or judgement and to ensure that it is carefully compared with the results. Such non-scientific phenomenon as extra sensory perception cannot be completely ruled out and even if it is improbable, if it does actually exist then to miss an opportunity to use it would be unforgivable. By the same token, to keep on making mistakes because of the irrational stubbornness of one individual is equally unforgivable. No doubt in industry, both mistakes are made, but probably more of the latter.

The obvious answer to this quandary is that of compromise. This means that an organisation should endeavour to move towards rational decision making but at the same time making sure that it is not neglecting talent which cannot readily be rationally explained. If this movement is not too rapid then extreme opportunities will not be missed. In any event, the introduction and use of a formal information and decision-making system cannot be accomplished overnight. It is a relatively slow process of logical analysis, testing and implementation.

A simple practical forecasting situation is now shown. In this case the system is forecasting for inventory control of a single product three months ahead. Demand for this product is supposed to be very sensitive to changes in consumer spending power—that is highly price elastic. The forecast, on the

6

basis of the formal model, indicates that the probability of the stock being exhausted for the given month is acceptably low. Suppose it is considered likely that a reduction in material prices could occur, and this would be reflected in the product price for that month. From past experience it would be known that a given reduction will result in an increase in demand with a known probability.

Hence judgements are required of the probability that the reduction will occur and given that it does, the probability that demand increases by a given amount. The original probability estimates concerning stock exhaustion must then be revised in the light of the new information. If this probability is still at an acceptably low level, then no extra stock need be ordered or manufactured whereas in the reverse case some adjustment would be necessary.

This simple example simply serves to illustrate how information and expert judgement fit into the overall model. In this case its use was in revising a forecast, but this is only one point in the general business problem or decision making procedure where judgement is required.

Check List

1. Has each problem been formally examined from the following points of view:
   (a) its principal parts and characteristics identified?
   (b) the information required clearly stated?
   (c) the information readily available analysed?
   (d) the decision alternatives available listed?
   (e) the different events which may occur listed?
   (f) the time and cost constraints on the collection of further information defined?
   (g) the probable effects of making alternative decisions assessed?
   (h) the most favourable alternative in terms of expected pay-offs selected?
   (i) the risks involved in adopting this alternative specified?
   (j) the alternative chosen considered in terms of company policies and objectives?
   (k) a feed-back mechanism set up to examine the outcome of the implementation?
   (l) the final outcome, favourable or not, evaluated to learn from both success and failure?

2. Has consideration been given as to whether expert judgement would help in any or all of the following ways:
   (a) estimating the severity of the problem?
   (b) deciding on its importance to the organisation?
   (c) assessing the extent of the information requirements?
   (d) interpreting analytical results and making hypotheses?
   (e) deciding on realistic alternatives?
   (f) deciding which of the possible events is either most likely or most relevant?

(*g*) avoiding serious omissions?
(*h*) setting priorities?
(*i*) deciding when to stop searching for information?
(*j*) allocating costs and time?
(*k*) interpreting the results of analysis?
(*l*) assessing risks?
(*m*) evaluating the value of further data?
(*n*) making subjective probability estimates?
(*o*) assessing the compatibility of the chosen decision alternative with overall objectives?
(*p*) choosing the right approach in implementation?
(*q*) assessing the personalities involved?

3. When using salesmen's forecasts have the following considerations been taken into account:
(*a*) the subjective nature of salesmen's judgement influenced by their function of getting orders?
(*b*) the importance of checking salesmen's information against the other sources?
(*c*) the possibility of assessing the reliability of a salesman's forecast over a period of time by comparing his previous forecasts with actual events?
(*d*) the requirement for salesmen to give numerical forecasts?

REFERENCES

Statistical Forecasting for Inventory Control, R. G. Brown, New York, McGraw-Hill, 1959
Smoothing, Forecasting and Prediction of Discrete Time Series, R. G. Brown, New York, Prentice Hall, 1963
'The use of cumulative sum techniques for the control of routine forecasts of product demand', P. J. Harrison and O. L. Davies, *Operational Research*, 12, 1964
'Comparison of different systems of exponentially weighted prediction', D. H. Ward, *The Statistician*, 13, 1964
Cumulative Sum Techniques, R. H. Woodward and P. L. Goldsmith, I.C.I. Monograph No. 3, Edinburgh, Oliver & Boyd, 1964

'Spectral analysis of seasonal adjustment procedures', M. Nerlove, *Econometrica*, 32, 1964

'Some techniques of short-term sales forecasting', B. V. Wagle, *The Statistician*, Vol. 16, No. 3, 1966

Short-term Forecasting, G. A. Coutie, O. L. Davies, C. H. Hossell, D. W. G. P. Millar and A. J. H. Morrell, I.C.I. Monograph No. 2, Edinburgh, Oliver & Boyd, 1964

'Forecasting sales by exponentially weighted moving averages', P. R. Winters, *Management Science*, 6, No. 3, 1960

Forecasting Seasonals and Trends by Exponentially Weighted Moving Averages, C. C. Holt, O.N.R. Research Memorandum No. 52, Carnegie Institute of Technology, 1957

Some Observations on Adaptive Forecasting, H. Theil and S. Wage, Report No. 6306 of the I.C.M.S. Econometric Institute, Netherlands School of Economics, 1963

Mathematical Trend Curves, An aid to forecasting 1964, J. V. Gregg, C. H. Hossell, J. T. Richardson, I.C.I. Monograph No. 1, Edinburgh, Oliver & Boyd, 1964

CHAPTER 4

The Logical Approach to Forecasting

THE ECONOMETRIC CONCEPT

All the models considered using time series analysis are very useful, but they each lack one important quality. This quality is an explanatory ability—that is they attempt to be prescriptive without being descriptive. There is no serious attempt to understand and evaluate the mechanism at work, if indeed one exists. While this 'black box' approach may very well work in many circumstances there must always be a danger that, for example, the 'historical trend' is not applicable to the future periods. This risk can be decreased if the forecasting model operates within a formal information system.

In some cases there may be opportunities for taking a more logical approach which may loosely be labelled the econometric approach. This is essentially the investigation, identification and isolation of causative factors and attempting to measure quantitatively the relationships between these factors and the variables under consideration.

The main purpose of this approach is to attempt to explain variation in the dependent variable by corresponding changes in the independent variables. In a sales forecast, the dependent variable is the sales data; the independent variables are those which are thought to influence sales—for example, price and marketing effort. The independent variables chosen are those variables which are thought, on logical grounds, to influence the dependent variable—the series for which a prediction is required. Hence it may be possible to construct a model—mathematical or otherwise, which formalises the hypotheses which have been made about the relationships which are thought to exist. This may then be used for drawing inferences about the dependent variable under consideration when the independent variables or parameters are allowed to change.

As a simple example of the type of situation in which this approach may be useful consider the case where a company makes bearings which are used in marine engineering. If these components are used in equipment which is installed towards the end of the shipbuilding cycle, it is possible that the published statistics relating to net new tonnage in, say, the United Kingdom could give a one or two year lead for the components. Taking the extreme case where the company is in a monopoly position, knowledge of the shipbuilding cycle may permit fairly accurate prediction for up to two years ahead.

In the less extreme case where the company has a part share of the market, it may be possible to determine the apparent relationship between net new tonnage and demand for the product. If the lag is long enough a good prediction may be obtained. If forecasts are required further ahead than the lag period[1] it may be possible to relate the new shipping series to some other variable also on a lagged basis.

There are a number of attributes which should be sought in establishing an econometric relationship. Again, time and cost constraints will often prevent the ideal from being reached. However, efforts to obtain these qualities will often be rewarded if only by a greater understanding of the way in which the company works or the environment within which it operates.

By far the most important characteristic is that it must be applicable to a particular problem or set of problems in a practical way—that is it must be relevant. In addition, the simpler the model, or set of concepts, the more easily will it be understood—not only by the constructor but also by independent experts who may not be well versed in the techniques of econometrics or are unfamiliar with mathematical concepts. This is extremely important because it is essential that the logic on which the model is based is subjected to whatever tests are available.

Another quality is that it should contain nothing which is

[1] Lag period is the time between cause and effect—for example if a company receives an order in March and delivers in June, the lag period is about three months.

theoretically implausible—this means that it should be consistent with both economic and statistical theory. If it satisfies this condition then it should follow that it should have an explanatory ability in that it should demonstrate relationships in a lucid manner.

A quantitative requirement of the model is accuracy of its coefficients, in respect to the problem which is to be tackled. If an approximate solution is sufficient then low precision in the probabilistic sense may suffice.

Again, depending upon the nature of the problem it should provide forecasting ability. If the model is a true representation of the actual situation then this will follow automatically.

A further characteristic is that of sensitivity.[1] It should respond to significant variations in observations from the levels predicted. Conversely it must not be over-sensitive and fluctuate wildly with random change.

Since the model is supposed to be as objective as possible, this implies that the subjective element is minimised. There will always be a subjective component and information relevant to this should be dealt with in a systematic manner.

The model's efficiency should be measurable—that is the time taken and cost of producing a prediction using the model. Further the model should be adaptable so that it changes to meet prevailing conditions.

As in the case of the time series models these conditions represent some of the major attributes which should be sought. This does not mean that a model lacking some of these characteristics may not be used; nor does it mean that further advantageous properties should not be specified and sought.

One last general point is that in building a demand model it might be tempting to consider one for say only one product in one market. While this approach would doubtless lead to the most detailed set of equations for a given quantum of effort, it is important to realise that most organisations require predictions for a wide range of products in different markets. Since

---

[1] Sensitivity is that the model is required to react to real changes in demand, compared with that predicted and to indicate that a change has occurred.

neither products nor markets are likely to be independent and although the complexity of the interrelationships may be very disconcerting, this problem must be faced. Hence the best approach may be a simultaneous one—of building segment models and at the same time an overall operating model. The immediate implications of this is that no segment model should be attempted unless sufficient resources are available to tackle the large scale problem. In theory this may be right but in practice the imposed limitations may not permit such an approach. Therefore an attempt should be made at the segment model, but bearing in mind that at some future date it may be slotted into the overall framework.

ISOLATING CAUSATIVE FACTORS

Identifying and isolating the variables which are most relevant to the series being studied are, in a sense, the most important steps in any econometric study. This is essentially because no serious attempt should be made to evaluate the apparent relationships which may exist until an understanding of their nature is gained. This in turn means that a logical analysis or assessment is required as a preliminary to any mathematical exercise. Although this is usually the case, there may be rare occasions when experience or prior knowledge is at such a low level, that the burden falls on the empirical analysis.

A simple example is where likely demand for a consumer product is to be predicted. If the product were say teenage clothes then future demand may in the first instance be predicted from the past relationships between demand and perhaps the population of teenagers aged between fourteen and nineteen years. (This of course can be predicted very accurately from birth and life statistics.)

It may also be postulated that demand is sensitive to price and that if margins were decreased, turnover would therefore increase. Hence the model builder could conceive a set of hypotheses as follows:

demand changes in some manner depending upon the absolute change in the population of potential customers;

demand increases when prices are decreased but decreases when prices are increased;

demand may depend upon price changes relative to price changes in competitive products;

demand depends upon other factors—for example current fashions, colour range available, durability, washability.

Clearly any one or more of the above factors may be sufficient to construct a reliable predicting model. Alternatively, other factors may exist which are much more important, for example the effect of advertising, but a start must be made somewhere, and it seems correct that the more obvious factors are considered first. It is also worth noting that if data is not available for one or more of the likely factors then the choice left to the analyst is restricted.

Thus, by a process of logical deduction based upon knowledge of the product and the environment within which it is sold, a set of hypotheses is formulated and these provide the starting point for the analysis.

The next step may be to examine the historical evidence or to undertake experimentation. In the example of teenagers' clothes the former is most likely to be applicable. If price were considered to be a major factor then a carefully controlled experiment using different prices in different areas could yield the required information. Alternatively, a well constructed survey may provide the desired data.

The examination of the past data is expected to provide evidence to support or negate the hypotheses formulated. In the teenage clothes example strong correlation may be found between year to year changes, or area to area changes, in the population of potential customers and fluctuations in sales. Alternatively it may be found that variations in sales are associated not only with the population movements, but also with price changes and economic cyclic effects. There may be a large number of possibly related factors and it may not be easy to establish whether association exists or not. A number of multivariate statistical tools exist for assessing association, and regression analysis may often be useful to measure the relationships.

There may be cases where it is impossible to carry out experimentation. The main reason for this is usually lack of time but there are other reasons—for example if a differential pricing policy is adopted it is unlikely to take long before the customers realise it. They may react by purchasing an alternative product or by purchasing the lower priced articles.

The opportunity for experimentation in marketing is limited, but if long-term attempts are to be made to understand the relationships between marketing factors such as advertising and demand, the practical application of the methods of experimentation will need to be explored. Certainly rapid and encouraging progress on agricultural problems has been achieved by using these methods.

The remaining approaches to isolating causative factors depend either upon the investigator's special knowledge or how well he is able to extract information from experts in a particular field. For example the marketing manager of a company producing microscopes may be able to indicate the factors which are likely to affect demand for the product, and this information may lead to quantified models.

THE CONSTRUCTION OF NON-MATHEMATICAL DESCRIPTIVE MODELS

Before attempting to quantify interrelationships it is useful to write down the hypotheses formulated on *a priori* grounds and the way in which the variables are expected to be related. Graphical methods are very often useful in helping to understand such relationships.

To demonstrate the way in which descriptive models may be used the following example relates to an attempt to build a simple model of the internal operating characteristics of a company. To simplify matters it is assumed that the company is an autonomous private company operating in an environment which is known to be stable.

Since it is a private company its financial resources will be obtained from the initial investment, retained earnings and short-term debt. It will not be able to raise long-term debt or issue equity, in general, because such a company is likely to be considered a risk. Other sources of finance such as credit, hire purchase, leasing arrangements and investment grants can be important but for simplicity are omitted in the following discussion.

Total assets of the company at any period may be considered to be a function of these sources. If the amount of the original investment is unknown it may be possible to write:

Total Assets = a function of — Cumulative retained earnings and Change in debt

Since the level of debt required, under given assumptions of growth required will depend upon the level of retentions it may be possible to write:

$$\text{Debt} = f \text{ (Change in level of retentions)}$$

where f stands for 'a function of'.

If the company wishes to grow faster than retentions will permit then it will use debt, but the level of debt it can raise depends upon the level of its retentions plus the rate of change in this level.

Sales will obviously depend upon total assets and also on margins, provided the market is sensitive to price.

Hence sales may be written as a function of these two factors, and since position in the economic cycle may also have a marked effect this may be included. Thus:

Sales $= f$ (Total Assets, Profit/Sales, Point in Economic Cycle)

All factors such as competitors, quality and other product attributes are omitted. Some may be included later, when the model is developed further.

Profits are derived from sales, but depend upon other internal characteristics, for example stock and debtor levels. Hence profits may be written as a function of these variables:

$$\text{Profits} = f \text{ (Sales, Stocks, Debtors)}$$

Finally retained profits will depend upon pre-tax profits, depreciation, tax payable and dividend payments. Assumptions about the last factor will have to be based on the historical evidence. The other factors should be calculable. Hence retentions may be written:

$$\text{Retentions} = f \text{ (Profits, Tax, Depreciation, Dividend)}$$

Since the last relationship yields retentions, this may then be used to estimate the following periods sales and profits.

Once this sort of exercise is attempted, very often when the various equations are brought together illogicalities will become apparent. There may even be an obvious omission of a variable or an equation. Following this examination it is possible to tentatively postulate the form that the equations may take.

There is obviously a very wide choice of ways in which relationships can be written or variables included or excluded. The prime consideration in formulating descriptive models is that they should be simple, logical and likely to approximate to the conditions which it is required to simulate. This is because the model builder is trying to utilise all his prior knowledge to provide a framework within which he may carry out his investigation.

If a simple descriptive model is constructed initially it is possible to approach an expert in the field for his views as to its likely validity. The model may always be made more sophisticated, and it is important to provide the right environment in which rapid understanding may develop.

If a more complex model is built up in this way it is necessary to examine its components—that is the individual relationships, and to consider whether the total effect of all the components together differs from the sum of the individual effects. In other words to attempt to find which factors are approximately independent and which are highly related.

Although the preceding example relates to some of the preliminary work in an exercise that turned out to be rather complicated, formulating descriptive models is a way of clarifying thinking by recording on paper the analyst's views as to the structure of the situation being investigated. The advantages are in fact two-fold; first it helps to sweep away some of the cobwebs, but even more important is that it provides a carefully specified framework for further action and for seeking other expert's views.

This latter point is important because no analyst can ever hope to have the insight of the specialist in that field, but at the same time the specialist is typically unable to focus his views or his knowledge as keenly as the analyst. There are many excellent marketing men who know their products, markets, customers and competitors very well indeed but do not have the training to focus their thoughts in numerical terms or probabilistic terms. It is therefore important that the specialist and the analyst should associate closely and by providing descriptive models the analyst may be able to utilise this association.

THE GENERATION OF INFORMATION REQUIREMENTS

Clearly, the precise information need is defined by the hypotheses which have been stated. The more effort which is put into formulating these, the more likely it is that the information need can be specified accurately. Hence the more efficiently may it be collected, if it is available; that is, at least the analyst has some idea of what he is looking for and what questions to ask.

As an example of the way in which the analyst can proceed the case of the company model is used. In order to test the relationships postulated it is necessary to collect data relating to the factors mentioned. In the case of a public company this may be accomplished by a visit to Companies House, or a letter to the company secretary to obtain several years' back copies of the published accounts. For non-public companies the information may not be available without the co-operation of that company's management.

Having obtained the required basic data the analyst may succeed in verifying that relationships exist in the form postulated. With considerable effort he may even be able to quantitatively evaluate these relationships. If he succeeds then he will have the basis of a good predicting model.

In one actual case where the approach was used with some success predictions were made for several years ahead. It became obvious that if the model were approximately correct the company was exhibiting incompatible aims. The apparent objective with regard to growth in turnover appeared to be incompatible with their apparent policy of growth in dividend payments. The level of retained earnings appeared to be on a downward trend with signs of accelerating downwards. From the evidence it was concluded that the company was very likely to face severe liquidity problems within two to three years if it continued on its current policies. It is unlikely that this view would have been formed if reliance had rested on conventional accounting methods.

Having formed this long-term view of the company's apparent instability, it was possible to ask the right questions to determine whether the apparent policies were in fact part of the management's conscious plans. It turned out that they were and indeed their management were aware of their impending liquidity problems. However, the value of the exercise was in providing the decision maker with advanced warning of a possible weakness in an acquisition prospect and providing the negotiator with some intelligent questions to ask.

One of the reasons why the acquisition was considered was because the company had a distribution network which could provide very strong synergistic benefits. The analysis indicated that this very strength was in fact a source of weakness in the sense that fluctuations in sales at the trough period in the economic cycle was associated with much more severe fluctuations in profitability. This was thought to be the 'pipeline' effect due to reliance on dealers. Reference to other companies which traded similarly showed that the effect was common. It was however necessary to assess its importance and again this provided the negotiator with some relevant questions to ask.

It cannot be stressed too strongly that if the approach outlined in this book is followed as a matter of general principle, the analyst and the businessman are more likely to provide better solutions to the problems they face. Their efforts should not be made in isolation and every opportunity should be taken to gather relevant information and consult the appropriate expert. One of the main advantages of working in a large organisation should be that there exists a wide variety of skills which may be called upon as and when required. The other main advantage is greater financial resources which may be considered in a similar way as manpower resources or special skills.

SOME ECONOMETRIC METHODOLOGY

The primary purpose of this book is to attempt to provide

middle and senior management, and perhaps also students of business problems, with a basic philosophy which is relevant to a very wide range of business situations. It is intended to create awareness of the potential which exists in the quantitative approach rather than specify, in detail, mathematical techniques. It is of course incredibly difficult to avoid some mathematics especially in a topic such as econometrics. It is also difficult to avoid using the jargon which has evolved since to those involved in the subject these expressions are part of everyday usage.

In the following account, an attempt has been made to reduce the frustration in the reader new to this field by relegating any mathematical exposition, however simple, to special sections. Jargon is avoided as far as possible; where special terms are used these are defined as carefully as possible. Many terms have highly specific meanings which need to be understood.

The basic relationships in econometrics are termed structural equations. As the name implies these describe the way in which variables change with respect to each other. A typical economic example relates to a set of equations which conceptually describe the relationships which exist between demand and supply for a product when price and tax varies.

These structural equations which show the basic relationships are known as the 'static exact case'. This simple model is a case which is said to be linear in both variables and parameters in the structural form.

By simple algebraic manipulation the equations may be expressed in terms of constants only, if tax is assumed stable, and these are known as 'reduced forms' of the structural equations.

Model I: The Static Stochastic Case

This model is similar to the static exact case except that it conforms more closely to reality by incorporating a stochastic[1] or random variable which represents unsystematic influences

---

[1] Stochastic variable is described by Carl F. Christ in Econometric Models & Methods as 'a variable whose different values on different occasions are determined as if by drawing numbers at random from a hat, there being a particular probability attached to each value'.

on the variable under consideration. Regression analysis is often used to analyse this situation and to estimate the relevant parameters.

In the simplest case it may be considered that demand for a consumable depends simply upon say the change in population, in a linear way. If the population increased by an absolute value of X, then demand will increase by an amount which depends on the product of X and a fixed constant.

The use of regression analysis to estimate the parameters depends on various conditions being met; for example assumptions about the underlying probability distribution, about serial correlation and other factors. In practice, many of the theoretical requirements may not exist and therefore the analyst must proceed with caution.

Model II: The Dynamic Exact Case

In comparative statistics, two static equilibrium conditions are often investigated in which all parameters and exogenous variables—that is those variables independent of the random variables—are alike except one. From such an investigation some view is formed as to the effect on the equilibrium values of the endogenous variables—that is the dependent variables—by changing the parameters, or exogenous variables, under consideration. Dynamic theory attempts to explain changes in the values of endogenous variables with time without necessarily referring to the structural relationship, or exogenous variables.

Such changes may be trends of one sort or another, for example, rates of change of variables or lagged relationships. One well documented concept is that of a system in a state of equilibrium which receives a shock in one period and responds to the stimulus in a later period. In this context the all important question is the length of the delay period and its distribution. An example of this is where government action at one point in time results in decreased consumer purchasing power in a later period and consequent reduced demand for a given product. Consumption depends not only upon the level of current income but also on whether it is changing or not. If government action results in falling income then consumers

7

will still react to their previous level of spending for some considerable time after their real income has fallen. This may be out of savings or increased hire purchase debt if this source is not blocked.

Such rates of change may be represented by differential equations if the time period is short and viewed as continuous. Alternatively if the time period is considered as discrete then difference equations may be used.

These difference equations are simply equations which contain lagged relationships.

QUANTIFYING CAUSATIVE FACTORS AND FORMULATION OF
MATHEMATICAL PREDICTING MODELS

To demonstrate how models may be constructed and relationships measured, an example is given which is of fairly general application. This is not intended as a case study and hence an over-simplified situation is considered.

Company X is a medium sized private company which produces and markets two main products. Both products are sold to a cross section of engineering establishments where they are incorporated into more complex products which are sold to a variety of end users.

Product A is ordered in small quantities whereas product B is ordered in large batches called off against a main order. Both products are reasonably competitive with respect to price and the company is considered to have a good reputation. Recent market research has demonstrated that trading conditions are stable.

The main problem is that product B requires a disproportionately large amount of productive effort compared with A, and the orders tend to arrive irregularly. The result is that severe loads are placed on the works in a fairly haphazard way and delivery period often lengthens. This may have adverse effect on the first product since the productive requirements are similar. Lengthening delivery periods are not acceptable to the user industry who may be more prepared to pay extra costs to secure a short order cycle.

The alternatives which face the management are:

should they restrict their production to meet average demand levels and allow delivery periods to lengthen from time to time hence losing business or goodwill;

should they maintain large stocks of product B so that production is held fairly constant and excessive customer requirements are drawn from stock. The cost of maintaining large stocks could be passed on to the customer in some cases;

should they introduce a production incentive scheme which will permit rapid changes in production—for example, by introducing three shift working or weekend overtime at very short notice;

or should they seek some optimal mix of any of the above alternatives.

The considerable over-simplification of the actual problem which faced the management helped to clarify the problem and this understanding permitted the specification of information requirements. The principal information required, if it were possible to obtain, related to likely demand for the two products and the way in which this demand might arise. In other words it was necessary to form a view of the long-term growth prospects for demand and also attempt to predict demand on a week-to-week and quarter-to-quarter basis.

In addition it was necessary to establish the expected costs, under differing demand assumptions, for the alternatives given. This meant calculating the probabilities, for example of the prospect of losing given quantities of business and the consequent financial loss. In this particular case some estimate of long-term damage was also attempted.

The object of this example is to illustrate the use of a demand model and the way in which it is formulated. No attempt has been made to reach a conclusion concerning the choice management should make.

It was considered that the best approach to the problem was to attempt to build both long-term and short-term forecasting models for products A and B separately.

Long-term forecasting models

Product A was first considered because experience suggested that changes in demand occurred relatively slowly. Since the delivery period required, and usually provided, was in general short there appeared to be no advantage in, say, considering orders in preference to deliveries or vice versa. Hence delivery data was used as this was most convenient.

The first step in the exercise was to extract from past records a series relating to deliveries made in each six-month period over the previous eight years. This period was chosen because it was sufficiently long to cover two general economic cycles and also there was considerable doubt as to the validity of the records before this date. The series was closely examined for any inconsistencies or misclassifications and an adjustment was made in the fifth period to allow for a severe fluctuation due to a six-week strike.

Having checked the data and satisfied himself of its validity the analyst proceeded to plot the raw data against time. Units, not values, of the product were recorded and hence no adjustment for inflation was necessary in considering real long-term trends.

Even though experience suggested that demand for the product was changing smoothly, the graph demonstrated periods of fairly marked fluctuation. In particular there appeared to be a cyclic movement which corresponded roughly with the economic cycle. In order to study the apparent trend more closely a four-period moving average was calculated and plotted.

As a first approximation a linear trend equation was fitted to the time series. A component was then incorporated to approximately simulate the periodicity of the four-year cycle. This equation appeared to approximately represent the overall linear trend and the apparent cyclical nature of demand.

The equation was used as a useful mid- and long-term predictor on the assumption that the underlying causative factors remained stable or changed at the same rate as in the past. However, it was a trend curve and hence failed to predict the fluctuations from trend which occurred from time to time.

This failure was reflected in the standard error[1] of estimate which provided for one year ahead a forecasting range of plus and minus 10 per cent at 95 per cent probability.

In fact this level of precision appeared to be good enough for the longer term investment decisions which needed to be made. However it was felt that some investigation should be made for the underlying factors since the model's validity depended upon these remaining stable.

To do this, the data was classified in each period by sales area and customer and the customers were grouped into industrial segments. The first classification produced nothing useful but the industrial classification yielded some surprising results. One was that currently 85 per cent of sales went to customers within two industrial sectors and another was the way in which these sectors had become important over the period considered. Both these sectors were in heavy engineering where the lead time between new orders for plant and orders for product A tended to be long. From conversations with major customers it appeared that the latter lead time was around six months to a year.

A Business Monitor series provided quarterly new order statistics for one of the sectors and the Monthly Digest provided monthly new order data for the other. Denoting these segments X and Z it was found that reasonably close relationships existed in both cases.

In the case of X there appeared to be no increasing trend in the value of new plant orders after inflation had been taken into account. However the order pattern followed the economic cycle roughly one year in advance of the product A and fluctuations in sales of product A were associated at least partially with variations in new orders of X. A further check with leading customers revealed that while their total market for this plant was fairly static in real terms there was a marked trend towards larger installations and these tended to require proportionately more of product A. This increase in usage

[1] The standard error is a measure of the predicting precision and is derived from the variance of regression. This in turn is a measure calculated by squaring the difference between the observed data and expected values calculated from the equation.

seemed more likely to explain the upward trend in sales of product A to this segment rather than the company increasing its market share. A plot of the data suggested that demand for the product was approximately related to changes in net orders for plant in the following way:

$$\log Y_t = a_1 + b_1 X_{t-2}$$

where X_{t-2} is net new orders on a two-period, that is twelve months, lagged basis.

A similar analysis and questioning of customers in segment Z suggested that new orders for plant preceded orders for product A by about six months. The apparent relationship in this case appeared to be approximately linear. The overall trend in segment Z appeared to be approximately linear upwards. From a graphical examination it appeared that sales of product A in this segment could realistically be represented by:

$$Y_t = a_2 + b_2 Z_{t-1}$$

One difficulty which arose was that the published statistics tended to be several months out of date when published. This was not too much of a problem for segment X but obviously was relevant to segment Z. The difficulty was overcome by asking key customers for their view of demand on a one-year ahead basis. This was not entirely satisfactory but allowed reasonably realistic inputs to be made.

If Y_{xt} represented demand in the t th period from segment X, and Y_{zt} represented demand in the t th period from segment Z, then the two predicting equations could be written:

$$\log Y_{xt} = a_1 + b_1 X_{t-2}$$
$$\text{and } Y_{zt} = a_2 + b_2 Z_{t-1}$$

Since sales to these two segments represented practically all of the sales of product A an approximation was used to predict total sales. This was formulated by least squares estimation and related total sales to new orders in the two segments. The equations was of the following form:

$$\log Y_t = a + b X_{t-2} + C \log Z_{t-1}$$

This yielded an excellent predictor on a three-months ahead

basis, not six months because of the delay in publishing statistics, and a good predictor for a six-months ahead period. For the second period, predictions were made by using a trend model for Z. For one year ahead predictions, estimates were made of Z on the basis of the trend model and these were checked against views obtained from the industry.

The model was placed on a computerised basis with up-dating and monitoring facilities. The computer then produced predictions at monthly intervals for periods up to one year ahead and the results were despatched to the decision points where they were required. The time series model was also computerised and predictions on this basis were compared with those made on an econometric basis. Naturally discrepancies occurred but the real role of the trend model was to make predictions up to five years ahead. The econometric model provided information on changes in the underlying factors.

This exercise was an important part of the total exercise because good predictors were found which permitted realistic estimates to be made up to one year ahead and hence removed part of the uncertainty which originally existed. No attempt was made at that stage to assess the affect of say decreasing or increasing prices at a rate above or below that which had occurred during the previous eight years.

The second part of this exercise was to construct a short-term model for product A. From a plot of the basic monthly data it appeared that a simple exponential smoothing model was applicable and various values of the parameters were assumed until a reasonably representative form was obtained. Since realistic forecasts were available at periods of three months ahead, these were used to judge the validity of the monthly estimates based on the smoothing model. Again the model was computerised so that results became available as soon as the latest data was fed into the program.

Producing a realistic predicting model for product B looked on the surface to be a more daunting proposition for the plotted data displayed very severe fluctuations which appeared to be random. As a start the same approach as for product A was tried and similar equations were constructed on both a time series trend basis and a rather unsatisfactory econometric relationship. The standard error of prediction was rather too large to provide a rational choice to be made between the decision alternatives. In a sense the model obtained would permit better estimates to be made than those produced by guesswork or those supplied by the salesmen. However the probability limits placed on the estimates made it difficult to select an optimal solution.

A closer examination of the mechanism revealed that main orders tended to be placed for a large quantity of the product and that deliveries would be requested at a few weeks' notice against the main order. It was found that most main orders related to a customer's specific contract and that all deliveries were generally made within one year of placing the main order. This in itself was useful for forecasting demand one year ahead but there appeared to be no discernible pattern within the year.

In an effort to ensure that an important point had not been overlooked, the analyst classified customers according to their industrial segment and cross-classified them by size of demand. Again there were difficulties because small customers often became important and vice versa, but this problem was partially overcome by allowing movement within the classification over time. Then for each such classification the distribution of the rate at which main orders were depleted was calculated. This was effected by dividing each main order into twelve parts, corresponding to months, and calculating the proportion of the total ordered at each period.

First of all it was found that small customers exhibited no apparent pattern. However large customers in specific industrial segments displayed a remarkable similarity in their pattern of calling off against the main order. By the same token the variation between segments was very substantial and this accounted for the marked fluctuations observed in the basic series.

Since main orders could therefore be classified into groups which were similar with respect to the call-off rate, the framework for a good short- and mid-term forecasting system was available. For each such group an expression was calculated which represented the proportion of a given order which would be called off by a specified time. These proportions were of course subject to variation and hence their standard errors[1] were calculated. From a knowledge of the order intake forecasts could be made up to one year ahead and the probability distribution of these estimates could be given.

A further refinement of the model was to incorporate a tracking and adaptive mechanism. For each main order at any given period the proportion ordered was compared with the forecast. If it were in excess of the forecast then future predictions were decreased accordingly. Similarly if it were less than the forecast then predictions for later periods were increased.

The result of the forecasting exercise was that a formal model was constructed and this was used to predict future demands on production. In addition to the system, an information flow was set up so that, if any important factor was determined in advance which could affect the forecasts, the estimates were revised in the light of the new information. Such information could arise from salesman feed-back relating to exceptionally large orders or any number of other factors.

Going back to the original problem it was now possible to choose the decision alternative which appeared most likely to yield the best expected return with a reasonably small risk of an unfavourable outcome.

PREDICTIONS AND PROBABILITIES DERIVED FROM ECONOMETRIC MODELS

If a formal model is used for forecasting, one of the advantages of it is that the forecasts may be made in probabilistic terms. For example it may be possible to make statements such as: 'The probability that sales of product A in period t will be above a specified value y is p per cent'; or alternatively 'There is a p per cent probability that sales of product A in period t will be within the interval x $\pm$ y.'

Even if estimates are made on a purely subjective basis it is still possible to specify these in probabilistic terms. For instance by asking the estimator to give his optimistic and pessimistic

---

[1] The standard error of the proportion p in a sample of size n is calculated from the formula—$\sqrt{(pq/n)}$ where $q = 1-p$.

view in addition to his expectation. This may be of some help but does not avoid the problem of built in optimism and pessimism which many people exhibit.

It is important to realise the importance of the types of statements indicated. At the risk of stating the trite, business situations are highly probabilistic. This in general means that although a decision may be taken on rational and well thought out grounds and in retrospect even appears to be the correct choice, there is always some chance that the actual decision outcome will be unfavourable. It is therefore essential, if decision making is to be systematic and consistent and successful in the long run, that the possible outcomes are specified in probabilistic terms. This makes it possible to evaluate the implication of each outcome and assess the expected effect. In addition it permits some attempt to be made at assessing the degree of risk involved.

The topics of probability and decision analysis are both considered in greater depth in later chapters, but it is important to make the point here otherwise such concepts as standard errors may appear to be meaningless in the context of practical decision making.

A standard error is in fact a calculated measure of the inherent variation to which an estimate is subject. For example, a linear equation relating demand for a product to some other variable may be written down as follows:

$$\hat{y}_t = a + bx_t \tag{1}$$

where $\hat{y}_t$ is an estimate of demand given the specific value of x_t.

The parameters a and b are calculated from a series of values of y each of which has an associated value of x. If the corresponding values are plotted against each other on arithmetic graph paper the overall trend may very well be linear but the individual observations will lie around a straight line rather than on it. Hence the above equation could be rewritten

$$y_t = a + bx_t + E_t \tag{2}$$

where E_t is a random variable and y_t is the observed level of demand.

The absolute magnitude of the E_t may be regarded as a measure of how well the line fits the data.

If equation (1) is subtracted from equation (2) it is seen that

$$y_t - \hat{y}_t = a + bx_t + E_t - a - bx_t$$
$$= E_t$$

Since $y_t - \hat{y}_t$ is the difference between the observed demand level, y_t, and that estimated from the equation, $\hat{y}_t$, it is logical to use this as a measure of the variation from trend of the data. The actual measure used for computing and other reasons is called the variance of regression and is simply the average of the sum of each such difference squared, that is

$$[(E_1)^2 + (E_2)^2 + \ldots + (E_n)^2]/(n - 2)$$
or $$[(y_1 - \hat{y}_1)^2 + (y_2 - \hat{y}_2)^2 + \ldots + (y_n - \hat{y}_n)^2]/(n - 2)$$

where $n - 2$ is the number of independent paired observations, $n - 2$ is used rather than n because two parameters are being estimated and hence there are only $n - 2$ independent pairs of observations.

The usual way in which the above expression is written is

$$\text{Variance of regression, } \sigma u^2 = \frac{\overset{i}{\Sigma} (y_i - \hat{y}_i)^2}{n - 2}$$

Note that if σu^2 is at or near zero, most or all of the observations will fall on the line and the variation expected in making estimates will be small.

In making a forecast it is usual that an estimate of demand is required for a value of x which is outside the range of the observation period. Such a process is called extrapolation and the variance of the extrapolated estimate can be calculated as a function of the variance of regression. The standard deviation of a series is the square root of its variance and the standard error of an estimate is the standard deviation of its expected value.

In the above case σu will be the standard deviation of regression but for a given estimate of expected demand it will possess a standard error. This will be in general different from the standard deviation of regression although derived from it.

To clarify this, the standard deviation of regression may be considered as a measure of the variation of all observations from trend. The standard error of estimate is a measure of the variation of that specific expected value.

For the two variable linear case see mathematical appendix, reference 6.

Since the probability distribution[1] of the estimate is specified approximately by its mean $(\bar{y}_t)$ and its standard error σy_t, the type of statement mentioned before can be written.

To the reader with some knowledge of regression analysis the preceding may be trivial while to the reader with no such experience it may appear complex. It is however virtually impossible to consider the topic of making probabilistic statements without indicating how these may be obtained. This necessarily requires an explanation of the concept of standard error. If this concept is understood by the generalist it puts him in a stronger position to specify his problems to the analyst more accurately and will help create a better understanding between the specialist or generalist and analyst.

One other concept which requires some explanation is the probability distribution. It is possible to estimate not only the expected value and its standard deviation, but also the shape of its distribution. For example, if it is a normal distribution then the probability of demand lying within a given interval below the mean is the same as of it lying in a given interval of the same size above it. Alternatively the distribution may usefully be expressed in cumulative form so that the probability of demand being above any given level can be stated. *Table 1* shows how this may be written:

Table 1

Event	Probability in % terms
Demand above £1·0m.	99%
„ „ £1·2m.	90%
„ „ £1·4m.	65%
„ „ £1·6m.	50%
„ „ £1·8m.	35%
„ „ £2·0m.	10%
„ „ £2·2m.	1%

[1] The probability distribution of the estimate is an expression which specifies the variation around the estimate and the shape that it takes—for example a normal distribution is a bell-shaped distribution symmetrical about its mean.

Clearly if the problem were to decide whether a new plant should be installed and it had to produce over £2·0m. of products then there is only a 10 per cent probability that it would. This usually would be far too high a risk to take where expensive capital equipment is involved.

However the manager taking the decision may feel intuitively, for reasons he would or could not specify, that the probability estimate was incorrect. He may think that there was a 90 per cent chance of demand exceeding £2·0m. Since the decision may be his responsibility there may be no alternative to letting him proceed. Indeed it may even be desirable that he should, but certainly he should be asked to substantiate his 'hunch'. If he could not, then it is essential that the outcome is observed and this consequence assessed. A company cannot afford to run the risk of losing a man whose intuitive judgement appears to be sound even in the face of an objective analysis. Similarly no company can afford a manager who continually makes decisions on irrational grounds and unfavourable outcomes occur. The point is that anyone can be rash if there is little or no personal risk in being wrong. Hence a very close scrutiny of such decision making with implied consequences, may deter the most reckless who might otherwise think that they have little to lose if they are wrong and perhaps a lot to gain if they are right. It is unlikely to deter, however, the man who genuinely believes that his view is right even though it conflicts with the evidence.

Evaluating the a priori information

In forecasting situations the *a priori*[1] information which leads to the formulation of a particular model is often assumed to be correct, but of course, in general this is not the case. Hence a means of evaluation is desirable.

Sometimes it is not possible to include all the initial information in the model—for example when some of the certain

[1] Again quoting Carl F. Christ 'Statistical inference proceeds, in its classical form, by starting from some set of statements, often called *a priori* knowledge of the model or the maintained hypothesis, which is accepted as correct and not questioned during the subsequent inference process'.

restrictions are of a form difficult to incorporate. One way to deal with uncertainty is to write down the subjective probability distribution that describes the state of prior knowledge and to build this into the estimation process. There are considerable difficulties in this approach but Bayesian methods offer the best potential for revising judgements in the light of latest information.

It is probably impossible to lay down a comprehensive set of rules for the evaluation of *a priori* restrictions. The general procedure is by means of formulating propositions, evaluating and revising these until the model obtained satisfies the builder on both logical and statistical grounds. This means that it is essential that as thorough as possible an understanding of the factors at work should lead to theoretical propositions about likely relationships. The available data is used to test whether these relationships appear valid.

THE ROLE OF ECONOMIC INDICATORS

Economic indicators have found fairly wide application in industrial forecasting especially in attempting to predict cyclical turning points in say a new orders received series. The approach is to look for an economic series or a composite set of series which in the past have exhibited cyclical changes in advance of the product under consideration.

There is no reason why in some cases such indicators should not exist. Indeed it is basic to the econometric approach that such series are isolated and that these have a causative effect on the series under consideration. For example, if a company is in a monopolistic position selling a component to an industrial segment it is very likely that demand for the component can be related to change in the user industry.

The important point is that indicators should only be used where there is some logical reason why they should have some such causative effect. If there is, then it may be far more profitable to attempt to measure the relationship and use this econometric model to predict future demand levels.

It is contended that indicators should not be used if there is no real supporting logic that a causative relation exists. This is simply because there are innumerable pairs of series which are correlated in a spurious way and there is no reason to suppose they will continue to move together.

If an indicator is found which is supported by logical considerations then in general it is preferable to measure the causal relationship. Hence in a sense the use of indicators becomes redundant.

There are many occasions when time and cost constraints may prevent a serious econometric investigation from being undertaken. In such cases the construction of a composite index or even a single series may very well provide some evidence for forecasting a year or so ahead. If the analyst has a good knowledge of the markets in which the product is sold he may very well be able to quickly unearth a series or set of series which do in fact indicate turning points.

It is important, however, for the analyst to start from his knowledge of the product and its markets. If it is a component or a product sold to an industrial user who then incorporates it into a product which is sold to a secondary market, it may even be possible to relate movements in the secondary market to changes in demand. If this is possible a long lead indicator may be obtainable.

One difficulty in finding indicators is of course that the lead period often changes and the analyst may only have available annual data. Hence it may be difficult to gauge the lead period with any degree of precision.

Check List

1. Has the mechanism at work in the market been examined with reference to the causative factors by:
   (a) investigating them?
   (b) identifying them?
   (c) isolating them?
   (d) their quantitative measurement?

2. Have the variables which have been extracted been arranged in order of importance and relevance?

3. Have the relationships involved been quantified?

4. Is the model which emerges:
   (a) sensitive?
   (b) over-sensitive?
   (c) objective?
   (d) of measured efficiency, i.e., relative to time taken and cost?

5. Have the following steps been followed?
   (a) a set of hypotheses formed based on knowledge of the product and the environment?
   (b) an examination made of historical evidence before the experiments began?
   (c) the major factors isolated by means of controlled experiments, e.g., price?
   (d) a clear statement made of the information next required?
   (e) verification established that relationships exist between variables in the form postulated in the hypotheses?
   (f) a quantitative statement made of all the variables in the light of new knowledge?

6. Have experts in the specific fields relevant to the model been approached for their views of the model's validity?

7. Have equations been formulated to represent the factors at work?

8. Can these equations be used to make forecasts with associated probabilities?

9. Has the forecasting system been set up on a continuous basis?

10. Have arrangements been made for forecasts to be adjusted in the light of the latest data?

11. Has a control mechanism been set up to monitor the forecasting system?

12. Are the results sent quickly to the decision makers who require them?

REFERENCES

Experiments with Input/Output Models, A. Gosh, Cambridge University Press, 1964

'An estimation of demand for cotton', R. M. Chatterjee, Paper at First Indian Econometric Conference, Calcutta, 1960

Economic Models: An exposition, Earl F. Beach, New York, Wiley, 1957

Econometric Models and Methods, Carl F. Christ, New York, Wiley, 1966

'Estimation of parameters in time-series regression models', J. Durbin, *Journal of the Royal Statistical Society*, Series B, Vol. 22, No. 1, 1960

Methods of Correlation and Regression Analysis, Linear and Curvilinear, M. Ezekiel and K. A. Fox, New York, Wiley, 1959

Econometric Theory, A. S. Goldberger, New York, Wiley, 1964

Econometric Methods, J. Johnston, New York, McGraw-Hill, 1963

A Textbook of Econometrics, L. R. Klein, Evanston, Ill., Row, Peterson, 1953

An Introduction to Econometrics, L. R. Klein, Englewood Cliffs, N.J., Prentice-Hall, 1962

The Role of Measurement in Economics, J. R. Stone, Cambridge University Press, 1951

Econometric Techniques and Problems, C. E. V. Leser, London, Griffin's Statistical Monographs and Courses, 1966

Econometric Analysis for National Economic Planning, P. E. Hart, G. Mills and J. K. Whitaker, London, Butterworth, 1964

Models, Measurement and Marketing, P. Langhoff, New York, Prentice-Hall, 1965

Regression Analysis, E. J. Williams, New York, Wiley, 1959

'Demand for cars in Great Britain', C. St. J. O'Herlity, *Journal of the Royal Statistical Society*, Series C, Vol. 14, Nos. 2 and 3, 1965

'The market demand for durable goods', R. Stone and D. A. Rowe, *Econometrica*, 25

Scientific Explanation, R. B. Braithwaite, Cambridge University Press, 1953

Logic of Statistical Inference, I. Hacking, Cambridge University Press, 1965

Logic of Scientific Discovery, K. R. Popper, London, Hutchinson, 1968

CHAPTER 5

The Essentials of Decision Making

INTRODUCTION AND LOGIC OF SYSTEMATIC DECISION MAKING

Decision making is a fundamental requirement of the management of any business organisation. Such decisions may vary from those of little consequence to those where the financial or other implications involved are considerable. Therefore, it is obviously incorrect to think that all decision making should be based on thorough objective analysis since in many cases the cost of making a wrong choice may be considerably less than the cost of carrying out a detailed study. A disproportionate amount of time is sometimes needlessly spent on relatively simple decisions whereas some major decisions are made rather too rapidly. Formal methods should be used in the important problems.

An explanation of the type of behaviour which leads to too much time being spent on simple problems and too little on the complex ones is required because it demonstrates a possible weakness in the human mental make-up. It is suggested that this weakness is the in-built preference of many people for concentrating on topics they can understand relatively easily, rather than trying to tackle complex problems which are not easily solved.

If this suggestion is correct then any technique which can reduce uncertainty or the complexity of a problem will enable the decision maker to focus his attention on the salient points. In most business situations of any importance there will be scope for the application of management techniques. However, this does not necessarily mean that a given technique will provide the best alternative to select. All it means is that the available information may be marshalled and utilised more beneficially and that a closer approximation of the probabilities involved may be estimated.

The bad businessman is almost certain to improve his performance if he familiarises himself with the formal techniques of decision analysis and uses these in dealing with the complex problems he meets. The average businessman will also improve his performance and is likely to learn more from his mistakes and successes in that he can always refer back to the assumptions and estimates he originally made. The good businessman is likely to improve his performance considerably because using these techniques should permit him to delegate more authority and concentrate on the longer term issues.

It is often possible retrospectively to carry out a post-mortem and conclude that the outcome of the decision made was good or even the best that could have been made. However careful the decision maker is in advance, he cannot guarantee a favourable outcome because of the uncertainty which is always present. At any specific time he always has the option of selecting an alternative, or gathering further information and, clearly, the more relevant information he gathers the more likely he is to select the best decision. Time and cost constraints will restrict the length of time which he can delay making the decision. Additionally, since decision making takes place in a dynamic business situation, events may be occurring which prompt the decision maker to change the estimates. Delaying decision making needlessly is often very bad policy because opportunities are lost, the decision often becomes more complex and, if the decision affects company personnel directly, these people may become frustrated and lose their sense of purpose.

The time spent ensuring that all the likely alternatives and events are considered is seldom wasted. It is one thing to ascribe a low probability to an event and then ignore the event, it is an entirely different matter if the event is not even considered. The sin of omission is probably the worst sin in decision making. Decision making may be improved at every level if the time is increased that is spent on thinking about the various events which might happen and the alternatives available. Decision makers are in no position to judge what additional information is required until they know all the reasonable alternatives which are open to them and all the possible events which might influence the outcome of their decisions. The off-course punter may, for example, be excused for backing the mount of the champion jockey only to find afterwards that the latter changed his mind just before the race and rode another horse. However, the on-course punter who selected the first horse from the morning paper on the same criterion should not miss the change.

Having considered all the possible alternatives and the various events which may occur the decision maker needs to assess the probabilities with which these events may occur and the affect each would have on each alternative. These effects are measured in time or monetary terms. However, there may be times when considerations other than finance are important. For example, in considering the future of an unprofitable operation the managing director may learn from marketing research that there is little market justification for continuing. If, however, there were strong sociological grounds for continuing he might decide accordingly. At least by taking a systematic approach he should be able to assess what this 'preference' is costing his company.

The decision maker is always concerned with evaluating the consequences of each of his possible acts in the light of the real state of nature. He must consider the probability of each situation occurring and make his decision on the basis of the affect of each situation on his possible acts and the associated probability. If the main criterion for deciding between alternatives is the profit motive then these affects need to be considered in terms of costs and profits associated with each act and each state.

If the fifteen stages shown in chapter 3 are followed and if the available techniques are used then the decision maker must become more systematic and learn more from his own experience. If the decision turned out to be wrong he should be able to spot whether it was just 'bad luck' or whether in retrospect he could have made a better decision. Bad luck here means an unfavourable outcome in spite of proper analysis and thought.

Most businessmen deal with their problems in a less systematic way, although they may implicitly consider many of the fifteen stages mentioned. The main reasons for developing a formal approach are to minimise omissions, clarify the objectives and permit the application of various techniques. The whole process is essentially aimed at reducing uncertainty and evaluating the consequences of specific events occurring.

THE EXPECTED MONETARY VALUE CRITERION (EMV)

A building sub-contractor will often need to submit a tender for a specific job and may not get the opportunity to requote at lower prices. Providing he can meet the specification of the customer he will usually obtain the order if his prices are below his competitors. Naturally this is an over-simplification because there are many other important factors—for example his reputation or the delivery date he is offering.

However, suppose the contractor estimates, from whatever information he has, that the probability of obtaining an order is p if he submits a tender at a price yielding £Y profit. In addition, assume that the costs he incurs associated with the tendering process are £X. There are only two outcomes in this case; the first that he obtains the order, the consequence of which is that he makes £Y profit, assuming his arithmetic is right; the second is that he is unsuccessful and the consequence is that he incurs a loss of £X.

Table 2 is a useful way of depicting the outcomes of the decision to bid at the price which yields a profit of £Y with a probability of p.

Table 2

Event	Probability	Conditional Monetary Value	Expected Monetary Value (EMV)
Win Contract	p	$Y - X$	$p(Y - X)$
Fail to win Contract	$1 - p$	$- X$	$(1 - p)(- X)$
			$pY - pX - X + pX$
			$= pY - X$

The table shows the two alternative states of nature in the first column with the associated probabilities of occurrence of each in the second column. The third column shows the net profit and loss conditional on the outcome of the tender and the last column indicates the expected monetary value. If the sum of these expected values (i.e. $pY - X$) is positive the decision will generally be to submit a tender at this price. Of course the price quoted will be sufficient to provide an acceptable return to the company or to meet whatever criteria are laid down.

The case discussed here is for illustrative purposes. In reality there will be a range of potential profits and associated probabilities and hence a bid will usually be made at that level which will bring the best return in terms of the expected monetary value criterion.

Although the E.M.V. criterion is very useful it does exhibit some weaknesses. One of these is that $pY - X$ is the same under constant conditions irrespective of capital resources available or many other applicable factors. If a company had very limited resources and the costs incurred in tendering for a contract were high, then it is possible that its management just could not afford to take the risk even though the E.M.V. was a large positive sum. For example, if a company had to make a decision in which there was a 10 per cent probability that they go bankrupt, even if there were a very high probability that large profits could be made, it is unlikely that the decision makers would put the company in jeopardy.

The extent to which a company or an individual will put to risk his capital varies from company to company, from person to person and probably even from day to day for the individual. It is a very difficult nettle to grasp and there appears to be no real analytical way around the problem at present. However, it ought to be possible for a company to develop criteria which include the level of risk acceptable in specific cases. This might be expressed as some function of their net assets.

Another weakness of the E.M.V. criterion is that personal preferences are excluded. For example, in the one man business example in chapter 2, the contractor may have preferred to do a particular type of work even though it was less profitable than other alternatives open to him. The E.M.V. criterion obviously cannot include preferences. However, the criterion can be used to select alternatives on financial grounds alone. Then these may be rejected in favour of one which carries less risk or is otherwise more acceptable to the decision maker.

THE ROLE OF PROBABILITY AND RISK IN DECISION MAKING

Both probability and risk are such important concepts that further explanation in greater depth is justified.

The assessment of the probabilities with which events may or may not occur is a key part in the decision making process. There are several ways of arriving at a probability estimate. In most cases in business it is a question of building up evidence until an acceptable conclusion can be reached. Clearly the amount of information required to convince some people is much more than others, but most people arrive at roughly the same conclusion given the same information. Otherwise verdicts in court would never be reached.

In everyday life it is normal to make judgements such as 'I think it might rain' and on the basis of the judgement take out a raincoat. These judgements might be based on cloudiness, or last night's weather forecast, or even whether the swallows are flying high. Although few people would want to waste their time by being so explicit as to say, 'I think there is a 30 per cent chance that it will rain,' this is essentially what is being thought.

Some business situations are as difficult to judge as the weather in England. In the same way that meteorologists study patterns of behaviour in the atmosphere and make forecasts on the basis of what is observed, the businessman must also study patterns and relationships. Such study may take the form of econometric investigations or it may be just unearthing the person who has the specific information required. Since neither approach can be completely relied upon, the combination of formal analysis and at the same time seeking out expert opinion is usually necessary.

If the sales manager of a company is asked how many items of a new product he could sell in the next twelve months, he might reply that he had no idea, if he knew nothing of the nature of the product or the markets in which it would be sold. If the product were demonstrated to him he might suggest that he could 'almost certainly' sell a small number of them and that he 'might' sell a larger number given that the price was right. He might even be persuaded to express his views in probabilistic terms.

A marketing research programme designed to estimate likely demand would provide further information which would lead to the sales manager increasing or decreasing his confidence in selling a given amount. After an intensive advertising campaign and the first three months results he will be even more confident that he will reach, or fail to reach, a given level of sales within the first year.

This increase or decrease in confidence is in fact an increase or decrease in his estimate of the probability with which the event will occur. If the marketing function is his responsibility he may maintain his confidence at about the same level by increasing or decreasing his efforts, giving his salesmen greater incentives or concentrating the marketing effort on one segment of the whole market. In this way his assessment of the probability of selling a given quantity may differ from that of a person not as involved in the mechanism which brings about the event. Yet the latter's estimate would usually be considered as less biased than the sales manager's and 'hence more acceptable'. The parenthesis is used because the absence of bias is not necessarily the best way to judge whether an estimate is acceptable.

To attempt to avoid this sort of difference of opinion in a highly subjective situation is often impossible and usually pointless. It is far better to turn a potential weakness into a strength by getting the sales manager to set his own objectives whenever his estimate is higher than the unbiased one. If he is given strong incentives to maintain his 'target' and penalties for failure he is unlikely to be over-optimistic.

The important point in this example is that where there is personal involvement in the mechanism which causes the event, the probability estimates may be different from those made by an unbiased person. In any case where profits or losses could be considerable it is advantageous to get estimates from both parties.

This shows how probability estimates might be obtained in a practical case. Clearly if the sales manager had estimated a low probability for his chances of selling a specific number of items and this was supported by research then the company might decide not to go ahead with production. The E.M.V. criterion may be applicable in making such a decision.

Suppose that the marketing research study confirmed the sales manager's estimate that there was an 80 per cent probability that the required quantity could be sold. Suppose further that this level of sales would yield a very desirable profit, then in normal circumstances the decision would be to go ahead. However, consider the case where the same probability of making the desired profit existed, but there was also a large probability of making a considerable loss. The company must have sufficient resources to meet this contingency if it occurs. If the company has insufficient resources then clearly management could not realistically think of going ahead, because failure may mean complete ruin.

Detailed company policy with regard to acceptable levels of risk would provide the necessary criterion. In the absence of such detail the individual decision maker would make his own assessment of the risk involved. Providing he has already applied the principles of decision theory he should be in a good position to evaluate the level of risk involved. Perhaps it is at this point, more than in any other business activity, where expert judgement has its most important role.

THE WORTH OF MORE INFORMATION AND OTHER COST CONSIDERATIONS

A key element in decision making is increasing confidence in the occurrence or non-occurrence of events which are relevant to the decision alternatives under consideration. Since the decision maker's degree of belief is dependent upon information it will usually be necessary to gather more information if his belief is to be strengthened. The process of gathering information, its analysis and interpretation normally takes time and incurs costs.

If the decision maker has to decide whether to install further capital equipment the critical event is whether demand for his product is going to increase or not. Since he is considering expansion it is likely that he already has some evidence to suggest that demand is increasing, for example, his order book may be increasing towards current capacity. He may therefore estimate that there is an 80 per cent probability that the extra capacity will be utilised. If he is able to calculate the cost of increasing production capacity he can calculate the profit he will make if it is fully utilised, or partly utilised, or the loss if it is marginally utilised. If he feels that a 20 per cent chance of under-utilisation is too high a risk he may initiate a study designed to determine the probability that demand will be within specified limits.

A survey of users may provide the answers he requires, but there may be a very large number of users and contacting them all would perhaps cost more than he would make even if his capacity were fully used. The problem is to estimate the probability that demand will exceed the new level of capacity and he may require this probability to be fairly high.

To be sure of future demand he would need to contact all users, if he could specify them, and find out their future requirements, if they knew them. As the cost of this information would probably be far in excess of the benefit of increasing his capacity, he may consider a first alternative of contacting sufficient to answer his question with 99 per cent probability. As an alternative he may consider contacting sufficient to be 95 per cent sure. Yet another alternative might be to contact in the first instance sufficient to be, say, 90 per cent certain of the level of demand and then, if necessary, to carry out a second stage to meet, say, his 95 per cent probability requirement.

Clearly each of these alternative approaches take a different amount of time and incurs different costs. Similarly the risks of expanding and failing to get sufficient work will be different in each case. The greatest loss would be the cost of the investigation. In the case where he was 95 per cent sure that demand is sufficient he obviously runs a 5 per cent risk that it will not be. Hence he could lose both the cost of the survey and the cost of unutilised capacity.

If costs can be estimated for each case he can calc
expected gains or losses and by using decision analysis
decide which is the best choice. A detailed example is
chapter 6.

Check List

1. In contract bidding have the following alternatives been realistically enumerated?
   (*a*) shall there be a tender at all?
   (*b*) shall the bid be high or low?
   (*c*) shall the bidding be for part of the contract only?
   (*d*) is a consortium bid with others practical?

2. Have the possible relevant chance events been specified? e.g., in the contract bidding case the different events that may occur may include different numbers of competitors bidding or specific competitors tendering:
   (*a*) the number of competitors?
   (*b*) specific competitors?

3. Has the structure of the problem been logically displayed?

4. Have all outcomes involved in each action when each event occurs, been evaluated?

5. Is sequential decision making required?

6. If so, has the relevant time horizon been ascertained and has the timing of future decisions been specified?

7. Has each estimate been supported by logical reasoning and has sensitivity analysis been applied?

8. Have the numerical calculations and assumptions been examined?

9. Have other factors such as personal preferences or risk acceptability been evaluated?

10. Have discounted cash flow techniques been used to assess the relative values of present and future profits?

11. Has the optimal set of decision paths been selected?

12. Has a value been placed on the optimal route?

13. Has a risk profile been formulated on the basis of the variation in the financial outcomes?

14. Has a sensitivity analysis been carried out to assess the degree of risk involved in possible variations in the inputs or the structure?

15. Has the sensitivity analysis been examined to assess how wrong the basic assumptions need to be, before another present alternative becomes more favourable?

16. Has the decision model been programmed so that the decision makers involved can carry out their own sensitivity analysis?

17. Has the formal analysis been so formulated that it can be used as a control system in the post decision phase?

18. Has a monitoring system been devised so that maximum learning is achieved?

19. Has an analysis been carried out of the degree to which the model fails to represent reality?

20. Having completed the model, has the analyst gone right through the system and checked on the inputs, especially subjective probability estimates?

21. If the analysis is to form part of a report, has the analyst adapted the presentation so that it is acceptable to general management?

REFERENCES

'Marketing research expenditure—A decision model', F. M. Bass, *Journal Business*, 36, 1963

Probability and Statistics for Business Decisions, R. Schlaifer, New York, McGraw-Hill, 1959

Applied Statistical Decision Theory, H. Raiffa and R. Schlaifer,

Division of Research, Graduate School of Business Administration, Harvard University, 1961

'The foundations of decision under uncertainty: An elementary exposition', J. W. Pratt, H. Raiffa and R. Schlaifer, *Journal of the American Statistical Association,* 1964

'Decision theory and marketing management,' R. D. Buzzell and C. C. Slater, *Journal of Marketing,* 26, 1962

Elementary Decision Theory, H. Chemoff and L. E. Moses, London, Chapman & Hall, 1959

'Perceived risk and consumer decision making', D. F. Cox and S. Rich, *Journal of Marketing Research,* 1, 1964

Decision and Value Theory, P. C. Fishburn, New York, Wiley, 1964

Decisions Under Uncertainty, C. J. Grayson, Harvard Business School Press, 1960

'Bayesian statistics and marketing research', P. E. Green and R. E. Frank, *Journal of Royal Statistical Society,* Series C, Vol. 15, No. 3, 1966

Research for Marketing Decisions, P. E. Green and D. S. Tull, Englewood Cliffs, N.J., Prentice-Hall, 1966

'Risk analysis in capital investment', D. B. Hertz, *Harvard Business Review,* 42, 1964

'Decision trees for decision making', J. F. Magee, *Harvard Business Review,* 42, 1964

CHAPTER 6

Some Underlying Principles and Techniques
Applicable to Decision Making

THE CONCEPT OF PROBABILITY AND DEFINITIONS

The essence of probability theory is in attempting to measure quantitatively the degree of belief that an individual or group of individuals have in the occurrence or non-occurrence of one or more events. The questions which require answering range from calculating the probability that a tossed coin falls 'heads' to a situation as uncertain as estimating the long-term profit potential of an acquisition candidate. These are two extreme cases and naturally different approaches are applicable. Before discussing in detail how probability estimates may be made, it is necessary to consider the various types of probability that may be used in practice.

The most common type of probability met in industrial production is that based on empirical evidence. This 'historical evidence' is usually the long-run stability of a sampling proportion. For example, in quality control of the continuous production of a component, inspection is often carried out on the basis of the observed historical level of defectives. Control charts are set up from historical data on the proportion defective, and no action is taken until the number of defectives, per say hundred items, reaches a predetermined level.

Another example of empirical probability is the determination of the probability that a six-sided die falls with ace uppermost in one throw. This can be achieved by tossing the die a large number of times and observing the proportion of times that it falls with ace uppermost.

If the die were tossed one hundred times and no ace appeared then the empirical evidence suggests that the probability of throwing an ace is zero and this would clearly defy common-sense. However, the result 'no aces' is possible, even though highly improbable.

If one ace were thrown this would suggest that the probability of an ace occurring is 1·0 per cent; similarly if five were thrown this would suggest a probability of 5·0 per cent. Again, if each of the throws resulted in an ace, the empirical evidence suggests that an ace is certain.

Since any result is possible, in the literal sense, the question which requires an answer is just how can empirical probability be used in practice? The answer is that although all the results discussed are possible, some will be very unlikely if the probability of an ace is a specified value.

Suppose, for example, that the die was loaded so heavily that only aces could occur, then clearly in a hundred throws, a hundred aces would occur. Since it is not known in advance that the die is biased, the experimental evidence is used to reach some conclusion about the required probability. This may be accomplished in a systematic way by assuming a specific prior probability and revising this on the basis of the empirical evidence. An example is given in the section on Bayesian methods.

Suppose, however, that the die were considered to be relatively free from bias. Then because there are six sides it may be concluded, without exact measurement or weighing, that the probability of an ace occurring in one throw is $\frac{1}{6}$ and hence if 100 throws are made, between 9 and 24 aces may occur. The reason why the number of aces is expected to lie between 9 and 24 is because this interval is equivalent to about 95 per cent of the probability distribution and hence 'less than 9' or 'greater than 24' are low probability events.

To explain this further, assume that the die is totally unbiased so that the probability of throwing an ace is $\frac{1}{6}$. The mean number of aces expected in 100 throws will be $100 \times \frac{1}{6} = 16\cdot7$, that is 16 or 17.

The probability distribution which represents this situation is known as the Binomial distribution, which has a mean of
$$100 \times \tfrac{1}{6} = 16\cdot7$$
and a standard deviation of
$$\sqrt{100 \times \tfrac{1}{6} \times \tfrac{5}{6}} \approx 3\cdot75$$

Since this distribution is symmetrical and very similar to the normal distribution, the range of the mean $\pm 2 \times$ standard deviations, represents an interval which includes 95 per cent of the distribution. Therefore, the range—16·7 $\pm$ 7·5, or 9 to 24 aces, will usually include the results of tossing the die 100 times. If a value outside this range is obtained, because of its low probability of occurring, it may be considered to be evidence that the probability of throwing an ace is higher or lower than $\frac{1}{6}$.

In the industrial situation it is often necessary to rely on the sampling proportion and therefore if in the case of a situation similar to throwing a die, the experimental result was a proportion of $\frac{1}{6}$, this would be used. However, the number of trials used to determine this proportion is important because in the case of 100 throws, even if the true probability were $\frac{1}{6}$, there still remains the chance that it is really $\frac{1}{5}$ or $\frac{1}{6}$. The realistic range of values is as previously calculated—that is between 9 per cent and 24 per cent.

Suppose however that 1,000 throws were made, then the expected number of aces is $1,000 \times \frac{1}{6} = 167$.

This time the standard deviation, given by the same formula is $\sqrt{1,000 \times \frac{1}{6} \times \frac{5}{6}} = 11{\cdot}785$, and the 95 per cent probability range is 167 $\pm$ 23, or from 144 to 190 aces.

This range from 144 to 190—that is a range of 46—in absolute terms is somewhat larger than that calculated in the case of 100 throws, where the range was 9 to 24—that is a range of 15 However, whereas the previous range was from 9 per cent to 24 per cent, in the case of 1,000 throws it is from 14·4 per cent to 19·0 per cent.

This shows that while the range in absolute terms gets larger, the range in terms of proportion converges towards 16·7 per cent.

To demonstrate this even further, in the case of 1,000,000 throws where the mean is $1,000,000 \times \frac{1}{6} = 166,667$, and the standard deviation is $\sqrt{1,000,000 \times \frac{1}{6} \times \frac{5}{6}} = 375$ the 95 per cent probability range is now 166,667 $\pm$ 750, or from 165,917 to 167,417 aces.

In this case the proportion may vary between 16·59 per cent and 16·74 per cent.

The conclusion drawn from this example is that in the long run, the sampling proportion tends towards the value which represents the probability of that event occurring. Clearly if it is possible to conduct one million trials under stable conditions, the probability measure obtained will be very reliable. In many business situations the opportunity does not arise and often estimates have to be made on the basis of a few trials only. Hence there will usually be a need for calculating probabilities by other means to support the empirical evidence.

The second type of probability may be termed *a priori* probability. This includes those cases where there exist say geometric or other scientific evidence which permits the calculation of the probability of an event occurring. For example, the probability that a six-sided die will fall with an ace uppermost can be determined from its physical properties. If the sides are measured with as high a precision as possible and these are found to be exactly equal and the centre of gravity is at the centre of the cube then each of the six sides will have the same probability of falling uppermost. However, to ensure 'equal likelihood' the tossing method must be unbiased and all other possible factors must act in a way which is neither prejudiced in favour nor against any of the sides.

If all the above conditions are met then there are six and only six possibilities, only one can occur at a time and all are equally likely. Hence the probability of getting an ace in one throw is $\frac{1}{6}$.

An industrial example of this sort of situation is when a company is putting out a tender for a contract. If the company knows that there are nine other companies bidding but has no knowledge at all of their likely tender prices, then they may all be assumed to have the same chance of being successful. Following this argument then the company may assess its own chances as 1 in 10. Suppose, however, that their market intelligence reported that they had found out the prices of all the other bidders and in each case they were significantly higher than this company's. If it was certain that the contract would go on a price criterion then the company's management would feel almost certain of getting the order. 'Almost' is used since there is always the small chance that the source of information was wrong.

The third type of probability takes the form of subjective estimates, sometimes called judgemental or personalistic probability. This type is often applicable to the often vaguely defined situations met in the commercial world and court-rooms. It is essentially a question of building up the degree of belief in the occurrence, or non-occurrence, of events from evidence which may include a little empirical information, may contain some *a priori* reasoning or maybe some combination of these and information which supports the view taken.

Taking as a specific example the evaluation of a prospective acquisition's profit potential, it may be possible to examine the past five or ten years financial data and determine the overall trend. This trend may permit an estimate to be made for five years' time which corresponds with an 80 per cent confidence level—that is, the degree of belief of the analyst is that there is an 80 per cent probability that the profits will exceed a given level. This view may be taken on the basis of analysis of the company's historical financial data alone and the 20 per cent risk of at least this level of profits not occurring may be too high.

An examination of the environment in which the company operates may lead the analyst to conclude that it is so attractive that it is almost certain that the company, providing it pursues past policies, will reach the level of profits required. Conversely he may find that the market is becoming increasingly competitive and pressure on margins is likely to have an adverse effect.

As the analyst probes deeper and deeper and gathers applicable information he will in general build up his confidence in the events occurring or not. In the worst situation, the evidence may be so inconclusive that he is unable to reach a verdict. In court an accused man in this situation would have to be found innocent.

The courtroom example is very illuminating because exactly the same process is followed in arriving at a verdict. There must be numerous cases of guilty men being pronounced innocent just as some innocent men are pronounced guilty. Examining this situation further, the pronouncement of a verdict of guilty is equivalent to the jury saying something like—'We are 99·9 per cent certain he is guilty.'

This immediately implies that there is a 0·1 per cent chance he is innocent and on this basis something like 1 in 1,000 innocent men would be pronounced guilty in the long run.

If the jury collectively thought that there was only a 70 per cent chance that he was guilty he would almost certainly be pronounced innocent. This is because the basic requirement is that the man is innocent until proved guilty—that is with something like 99·9 per cent certainty.

It is pertinent to note that in a sense probability is a 'personal' matter. It depends upon the amount of information a person has in his possession and to what extent his information differs from his colleagues or the world at large. In a horse race between two horses one is backed at 10 to 1 on— that is a probability of winning of 90 per cent—and the other at 7 to 1 against—that is a probability of winning of 12·5 per cent. Clearly the consensus of opinion of the punters and racing fraternity is that the favourite has a chance of losing, a little greater than one in ten. If the favourite were doped or ill, or the jockey bribed, or if he makes a bad mistake the horse may lose. In either the case of being ill or a bad mistake by the jockey this may be regarded as bad luck corresponding with the one in ten chance of losing. In either of the corruption cases a few people will know with a high degree of certainty that the favourite will lose.

Another form of probability is known as inverse probability and is derived from Bayes' Theorem. Suppose an event never occurs unless it is preceded by one or the other of some set of events. If the event is known to have occurred then the chance that it was preceded by a particular one of the other events is calculable. The way in which this may be done is explained in a later section on the Bayesian approach.

In manipulating probabilities and for further understanding there are several basic rules. The simplest refers to the situation where the marketing manager allocates a probability of p to the event that he will secure a particular order. The only possible alternative event is that he will fail and this automatically has the probability of $q = 1 - p$. If he is 90 per cent certain he will get the order then the implication is that there is a 10 per cent chance he will fail. If only these two 'mutually exclusive' events are possible and one must occur, then $p + q = 1$.

A slightly more complex case is where there are two contracts available, called contract A and contract B, to which the marketing manager assigns probabilities of success of $p(A)$ and $p(B)$ respectively, where $p(A)$ is his probability of securing contract A, and $p(B)$ is his probability of securing contract B. The probability that he gets both is

$$p(A) \times p(B)$$

If he allocates numerical values to these probabilities, for example

$$p(A) = 0.9$$
$$p(B) = 0.8$$

then his probability of getting both contracts is

$$p(A) \times p(B) = 0.9 \times 0.8, \text{ or } 72 \text{ per cent certain}$$

Since the probability of getting contract B is $p(B) = 0.8$, then the probability that he fails to get contract B is $1 - p(B) = 1 - 0.8 = 0.2$.

If this probability is denoted by $p(\bar{B})$, where $\bar{B}$ means the event 'not getting contract B', then if he were interested in getting only contract A this implies that B fails to occur and the probability of this joint event is

$$p(A) [1 - p(B)] = p(A) \times p(\bar{B}) = 0.9 \times 0.2 = 18 \text{ per cent}$$

Similarly if $p(\bar{A})$ represents the probability of 'not getting contract A' then the probability of getting contract B but not A is

$$p(B) [1 - p(A)] = p(B) \times p(\bar{A}) = 0.8 \times 0.1 = 0.08 \text{ or } 8 \text{ per cent}$$

Finally, there remains one event to be evaluated. This is the joint event 'fail to get contract A and fail to get contract B'; which is represented by

$$[1 - p(A)] \times [1 - p(B)] = p(\bar{A}) \times p(\bar{B}) = 0.1 \times 0.2 = 0.02$$

Summarising these events, there are four distinct cases and the sum of the probabilities equals unity, since one of the four must happen

Event	*Probability*

Win Contract A and Contract B
$$p(A) \times p(B) = 0.9 \times 0.8 = 0.72$$
Win Contract A but lose Contract B
$$p(A) \times p(\bar{B}) = 0.9 \times 0.2 = 0.18$$
Win Contract B but lose Contract A
$$p(B) \times p(\bar{A}) = 0.8 \times 0.1 = 0.08$$
Lose Contract A and Contract B
$$p(\bar{B}) \times p(\bar{A}) = 0.1 \times 0.2 = \underline{0.02}$$
$$\underline{\underline{1.00}}$$

If the marketing manager wished to estimate the probability of getting at least one order, he only needs to consider the sum of the first three results which is the same as 1 minus the probability that he wins no order

$$1 - p(\overline{A}) \, p(\overline{B}) = 0.98 \tag{1}$$

Since $p(\overline{A}) = 1 - p(A)$ and $p(\overline{B}) = 1 - p(B)$ then the above expression, equation (1) can be written

$$1 - [1 - p(A)] \times [1 - p(B)]$$

If this is expanded the expression becomes

$$1 - [1 - p(B) - p(A) + p(A) \times p(B)]$$

which equals

$$p(A) + p(B) - p(A) \times p(B) \tag{2}$$

Equation (2) gives the probability that at least one of the two events A and B occur, and is known as the 'addition law of probability'. Reference 7 of the mathematical appendix develops the addition law of probability for any number of events, and reference 8 describes the multiplication law of probability.

A more practical case would be where the marketing manager has a possible twenty different contracts each having different probabilities of success and differing substantially in value. If these will all be decided upon within the next month and will then provide work for the following three months, then he would want to assess the amount of work he is likely to get and arrange production accordingly. Supposing he wished to be 90 per cent sure of getting a particular level of work, then he could calculate this from the individual probability estimates, following exactly the same principle as in the last example.

To record all the possibilities in a twenty-contract case would be far too lengthy, but the results are calculated for a four-contract case. These contracts, denoted A, B, C and D, are of value £1,000, £5,000, £10,000 and £15,000 and the probabilities allocated to each are 0·9, 0·8, 0·7 and 0·6 respectively. There must be a total of sixteen different events corresponding with 'all fail', getting only one contract, winning two, losing only one, losing none. The probabilities of these different events and the consequent values of work are shown in *Figure 11* Also shown is the approximate expected value of work which would be obtained.

Clearly he is $1 - 0.0024 = 99.76$ per cent certain of getting at least one, and 96 per cent certain of getting at least two. Alternatively he has a probability of about 83 per cent of getting orders worth £15,000 or above but only 56 per cent of getting business worth £20,000 or more.

Another important concept in probability theory is the notion of conditional probability (see reference 9 in the appendix). If it is known that one event has already occurred what then is the probability of a second event occurring? Clearly if the two events are completely independent then the occurrence of one will have no effect whatsoever on the other.

In this example the contracts or marketing manager may be concerned with obtaining orders of value £15,000 or more. If he learnt that he had already secured contract D (£15,000) then he would know that he had met his objective—in other words the probability of the event '£15,000 or more orders' is revised from 0.83 to 1.00. If he learnt that the order value was £10,000 —that is contract C—then the probability of his reaching his

Event	Probability		Value	$E(X)$
Get all four (i.e., A, B, C and D)	$0.9 \times 0.8 \times 0.7 \times 0.6 = 0.3024$		£31,000	9374.4
Get A, B and C	$0.9 \times 0.8 \times 0.7 \times 0.4 = 0.2016$		£16,000	3225.6
„ A, B and D	$0.9 \times 0.8 \times 0.3 \times 0.6 = 0.1296$		£21,000	2721.6
„ A, C and D	$0.9 \times 0.2 \times 0.7 \times 0.6 = 0.0756$		£26,000	1965.6
„ B, C and D	$0.1 \times 0.8 \times 0.7 \times 0.6 = 0.0336$		£30,000	1008.0
„ A and B	$0.9 \times 0.8 \times 0.3 \times 0.4 = 0.0864$		£6,000	518.4
„ A and C	$0.9 \times 0.2 \times 0.7 \times 0.4 = 0.0504$		£11,000	554.4
„ A and D	$0.9 \times 0.2 \times 0.3 \times 0.6 = 0.0324$		£16,000	518.4
„ B and C	$0.1 \times 0.8 \times 0.7 \times 0.4 = 0.0224$		£15,000	336.0
„ B and D	$0.1 \times 0.8 \times 0.3 \times 0.6 = 0.0144$		£20,000	288.0
„ C and D	$0.1 \times 0.2 \times 0.7 \times 0.6 = 0.0084$		£25,000	210.0
„ A only	$0.9 \times 0.2 \times 0.3 \times 0.4 = 0.0216$		£1,000	21.6
„ B only	$0.1 \times 0.8 \times 0.3 \times 0.4 = 0.0096$		£5,000	48.0
„ C only	$0.1 \times 0.2 \times 0.7 \times 0.4 = 0.0056$		£10,000	56.0
„ D only	$0.1 \times 0.2 \times 0.3 \times 0.6 = 0.0036$		£15,000	54.0
Get none	$0.1 \times 0.2 \times 0.3 \times 0.4 = 0.0024$		ZERO	0.0
	Total 1.0000			20,900.0

Figure 11

THE CONCEPT OF CONDITIONAL PROBABILITY

target would be revised upwards. In fact only the occurrence of event 'A only' would result in failure and hence his probability of success becomes about 93 per cent certain. This is calculated as shown in *Figure 11*.

Since contract C has been awarded, there are only three left—contracts A, B and D, valued £1,000, £5,000 and £15,000, with associated probabilities of 0·9, 0·8 and 0·6 respectively.

Since now, failure to achieve the £15,000 objective can only occur if the following event happens

Win contract A and no other

then the revised probability of maintaining the objective is calculable.

For the probability of the event is

$$0.9 \times (1 - 0.8) \times (1 - 0.4) = 0.072$$

Hence the probability of this adverse event not occurring is $1 - 0.072$ about 93 per cent.

FORMULATING HYPOTHESES

Formulating hypotheses is fundamental to the business of decision making, because at most of the fifteen stages listed on page 58 the decision maker is either implicitly or explicitly doing just that. For example having clarified the problem and identified its principal parts and characteristics the decision maker starts thinking about the information he needs. This information requirement is a direct result of his having considered that there is some chance of specific events occurring. If he wished to be truly systematic in his approach he could allocate probabilities to these considerations and gather information until he was sufficiently confident of the outcomes in which he is interested.

In a more general sense the decision maker uses his experience or current information to draw tentative conclusions or hypotheses which he wishes to examine further. He then proceeds with making observations, gathering further information or experimentation until he is able to reject the hypotheses or is reasonably satisfied that they are supported by the evidence.

The concept of hypothesis formulation is very closely tied up with the evaluation of probability and the occurrence of the events considered by the hypothesis is usually expressed in probabilistic terms. Indeed the hypothesis itself may also be considered in probabilistic terms.

Suppose the market analyst of a company, which produces a product used in several different industrial sectors, is attempting to build a mid- or long-term forecasting model for the product. He may proceed by determining which sectors are relevant and of these which are the most important. He may go further and hypothesise that sales for his product will depend on a lagged basis on the activity in these sectors. If the product is a component used in capital equipment, for example marine bearings used in shipbuilding, he may measure sector activity by the level of new orders for that equipment.

It sometimes happens that in the case where a strong relationship is expected a good econometric relationship cannot be formulated, either because the logic or data is poor or because of unidentified factors. Similarly there are cases where although the logic is not very good, strong empirical relationships appear. In the sense of hypothesis testing it is perhaps best to consider both 'logical evidence' and empirical evidence together and where the latter supports the former the relationship derived may be of considerable use. If there is strong empirical evidence but the logic or economic theory is not clear then there are obvious dangers involved in using the relationship for predicting. There are many examples of highly correlated variables which are quite spurious.

Take, as a highly simplified example, the prediction of bearings to be used in shipbuilding. Suppose the company has a very large market and suppose that the value of bearings that a ship requires is roughly proportionate to its size. Then it would appear that demand for these marine bearings could be calculated from the known tonnage on order at any given time. An examination of past data may show that sales and net new tonnage move in roughly the same direction at about a one year lag, but that the relationship was not so good as would be expected. This might require a revision of the hypothesis that there exists a good relationship. The analyst might hypothesise that the length of lag may depend upon the size of the ships being built. If he were able to obtain suitable information he might then attempt to relate sales of the product not to total shipbuilding but the components of the total which showed greatest correlation. In this way he may get a better relationship in empirical terms and one which also satisfies logical considerations.

He may have observed that sales of the component were highly correlated with some other variable, for example Gross National Product. Although he may not be able to provide a very good argument to support the apparent relationship, in the absence of any other he may use it with caution to predict likely future demand.

The case of determining the probability of throwing a head with a penny is a good academic example of the sort of procedure required; if nothing is known of the coin then the hypothesis would be that the probability of a head is 0·5. If the coin were thrown in an unbiased way one hundred times and the number of heads counted and found to be 40 then this is evidence to reject the original hypothesis and possibly replace it with one that the coin is biased in favour of tails. Just how much evidence this result provides can only be considered in terms of how unexpected the result may be. If 49 heads had been thrown this would probably not be taken as grounds that the coin was biased. In fact it can be calculated that the probability of throwing as few as 40 or less is only about 2 per cent if the coin were unbiased. Hence the evidence may be considered sufficient in some circumstances to reject the original hypothesis in favour of one which allocated a higher probability to the result being tails. The amount of evidence required in any particular case depends entirely upon the consequences of making a wrong decision. Clearly there are two types of errors which may be made; the first is to reject a hypothesis on the basis of the evidence when it is in fact true and the second is to accept it when it is in fact false.

In general there will be costs involved when such errors are made since the decision alternative chosen will generally depend upon the particular hypotheses selected. In the business situation where experimentation is frequently impossible and making observations or gathering sound information is hazardous it is often difficult to weigh the evidence as carefully as in the example. The probability estimates involved may very well be the combination of both empirical and subjective evidence and hence conclusions will often be more difficult to reach. However the discipline and practice of expressing hypotheses in numerical probabilistic terms and revising these on the basis of new information is bound to help the decision maker to become more systematic. In addition he can always record the main reasons why he selected particular values and his reasoning may be examined independently by colleagues for its validity.

Naturally where subjective probability estimates are made their values depend not only upon the available evidence but also upon the particular personal circumstances of the executive involved. If he has to make a decision where the wrong choice would cost the company a considerable sum then his career could receive a setback. Hence in such a case he may tend to be ultra-cautious. Such caution, or possible recklessness on the part of someone with little to lose, may result in poor decision making. The way to deal with this problem is to employ well trained mature management—mature in the sense that decisions are seen to be made probabilistically. In addition, wherever a subjective probability estimate is made the reasons for the selection of that value should be given specifically, so that senior management will have the opportunity of reassessing the estimate in the light of their own knowledge or wider view. In any case where a particular estimate can have substantial effects, efforts should always be made to determine whether further applicable information can be obtained and whether its cost is warranted.

The consequence of adopting this routine is that each critical point in the decision-making process comes under close scrutiny and the estimate is either maintained or adjusted. Further, by including the reasons why a specific estimate was made the executive is compelled to be as objective as possible.

INTRODUCTION TO THE BAYESIAN VIEWPOINT (INVERSE PROBABILITY)

The Bayesian approach is particularly relevant to the problem of using subjective probability estimates in decision making.

The approach permits the revision of such prior judgements in a systematic way as the evidence is compiled. In practice the application of Bayesian methods has not been developed very far although the potential exists. Bayes' Theorem is given in the appendix, reference 10.

The type of situation where the Bayesian viewpoint is applicable occurs typically when the decision maker is faced with a number of alternatives the consequences of which are not known with certainty. Costs are associated with selecting the wrong alternatives and the decision maker always has the option to acquire further information to decrease the uncertainty involved, but this process will also usually incur costs.

The Bayesian technique may help to determine how much additional information is required and what alternative the decision maker should select. In this approach a probability may in fact be allocated to the hypothesis itself rather than the subject matter of the hypothesis. The previous section demonstrated the classical approach of formulating an hypothesis and accepting or rejecting it on the basis of the acceptable risk of rejecting it when it is true or accepting it when false. The Bayesian method is applicable to the probability of the hypothesis being of belief of the decision maker in the true or false and provides a mechanism for revising the degree validity or otherwise of the hypothesis. Bayesian analysis has been described as a prescriptive technique for the consistent decision maker.

The first step in using Bayesian analysis is to allocate prior probabilities to the occurrence of the events which are thought to be relevant. Prior Analysis[1] is the term given to the selection of the decision alternative on the basis of prior probabilities alone—that is using the expected value criterion as previously explained, (p. 118).

The second stage is termed Posterior Analysis[2] and is

[1] P. E. Green and R. E. Frank in 'Bayesian statistics and marketing research' in the *Journal of the Royal Society of Statisticians*, Vol. XV, No. 3 define Prior Analysis as 'the manner in which a terminal act is chosen on the basis of prior probabilities alone' and the decision alternative chosen on the basis of the expected value criterion.

[2] Posterior Analysis is described by the same authors as 'the manner in which a terminal act is chosen on the basis of combined prior and experimental evidence.'

concerned with the way in which an alternative is chosen on the basis of prior information and further evidence. The prior probabilities are modified by Bayes' Theorem with reference to the later information.

The third stage is called Preposterior Analysis[1] and is concerned with the evaluation of alternative strategies.

As an example of the use of the Bayesian approach, a manufacturer may have to decide whether or not to introduce a new product. He may make the decision on his present knowledge— that is prior analysis, or he may consider various strategies for gathering further information. Essentially, he needs to know if demand for the product will be sufficient to make its introduction worthwhile. He could choose to commission a full-scale market study at a known cost and get more or less 'certain' information. Alternatively he could undertake a limited sample survey and be less sure that demand is sufficient but at a lower cost. He may even commission multi-stage investigations where the decision to carry out a second or third stage would depend upon the results of the first or second. Providing he knows the approximate cost of the different alternatives and the level of confidence associated with each then he may be able to use Bayesian methods to help make a rational choice.

A formal definition of Bayes' Theorem is given in reference 10 of the appendix.

A non-practical example is used to demonstrate how Bayes' Theorem may be used to modify the degree of belief in a situation as experimental evidence accumulates.

Suppose that a gambler entered a casino and watched the roulette wheel. If he were asked to estimate the probability that the wheel was so heavily biased that black would never occur he might reply that it was extremely improbable. He may go further and say that the probability was less than one in a million.

The problem is to determine how this prior probability (1 in 1,000,000) might be revised in the light of experimental evidence. Clearly if black appeared then the wheel would

[1] P. E. Green and R. E. Frank then define Preposterior Analysis as 'the manner in which possible strategies (involving information collection and terminal action) are evaluated.'

obviously not be so biased. However, if black fails to occur in ten or twenty successive results how would this affect the gambler's prior degree of belief?

If the wheel were really biased then the probability of getting 10 non-blacks in succession would be unity—that is certain to occur. If the wheel were unbiased then the probability of getting 10 non-blacks in succession would be around $(\frac{1}{2})^{10}$— that is assuming that if the wheel is unbiased the probability of black occurring in any one spin is $\frac{1}{2}$.

From Bayes' Theorem the revised probability of an event given the experimental evidence can be calculated from the prior and conditional probabilities.

In this case the prior probability is 1/1,000,000 and the conditional probabilities are:

(*a*) Certainty (i.e. 1)—given that it is biased.

(*b*) $(\frac{1}{2})^{10}$—given that it is unbiased.

The probability that the wheel is biased, on the experimental evidence, is therefore:

$$\frac{\dfrac{1}{1,000,000} \times 1}{\dfrac{1}{1,000,000} \times 1 + (1 - 0\cdot000001) \times (\frac{1}{2})^{10}} \approx \frac{1}{1,000}$$

In other words the experimental evidence permits the revision of the prior probability from one millionth to about one thousandth. This is just on ten successive results.

The result depends upon two things—the degree of belief the gambler has to start with and the quantity of experimental evidence observed.

In the business situation the decision maker consciously or not uses his judgement in assessing the probability distribution of a random variable. Hence he may consider the distribution of past demand for a product and project this forward to obtain estimates of future demand modified by his judgement. As further information reaches him he revises his prior judgement and increases or decreases the estimates of future demand.

The Bayesian approach may be applicable in formalising such revisions and no doubt in due course standard methods will become available.

DECISION TREE TECHNIQUE

Some examples of decision trees have already been given. In chapter 2, the elements of the approach to business problem solving were laid out in stages. It was mentioned that it is essential that all realistic decision alternatives should be written down and all possible events that can react with any of the alternatives must be considered. This consideration requires not only the estimation of the probabilities with which they will occur but also the evaluation of the financial outcomes which will be obtained if a particular act is chosen.

The decision tree as shown in the sketch on p. 44 is a graphical representation of this statement. It is now a fairly accepted convention that present decision points are shown on the left of the diagram and are denoted by squares. Similarly the events which may occur are denoted by circles and are usually related to the appropriate decision alternatives by straight lines. Still reading from left to right, lines, or decision paths, go from the events to future decisions, again represented by squares. These decisions may be termed second order or second stage decisions. The process continues until a sufficient time horizon has been considered. Finally on the right hand side of the diagram, the outcomes of each of the decision/event paths[1] are shown.

Such representation permits the logical consideration of the decision process. It shows the various events which may occur and the decisions which may have to be made and can therefore be examined independently for omissions of possibly important alternatives or events. It is also possible to examine it for sequential errors. In addition, once a satisfactory representation of the practical situation is completed, it becomes more obvious what the information needs will be.

The complexity of the tree can be increased considerably by including the less important details, but such complexity can be extremely confusing if the analyst or the businessman is not experienced in using the technique. To avoid confusion it is

---

[1] A decision/event path is a set of sequential decisions and events where a decision needs to be made now and this is followed by a specific event which leads to a later decision and so on until a 'pay-off' is reached.

better to compromise and omit the detail. The tree will then show the main alternatives and the detail can be dealt with in the accompanying analyses. As experience is gained in handling the technique, the tree can be split into different parts.

Having shown alternatives, events and outcomes, the next step is to record on the tree the following numerical information:

(a) the cost of implementing each decision

(b) the probability of each first stage event occurring

(c) the conditional probability of later events occurring

(d) the financial outcome of each decision path.

Decision alternatives which are redundant because of corporate preferences or risk limitations, are still included in the analysis just as if they were real alternatives. However, the decision path is marked with a / to denote its redundancy. The point of including these is to evaluate the 'opportunity cost' of the preference.

Although the decision tree permits the numerical evaluation of the alternatives before the decision maker, this is only part of its value. Even more important is the way it can be used to show the structure of the problem and hence pinpoints the need for further information, and probability estimates. It may not provide the 'best alternative' since in the last resort the preference of the decision maker, or the corporation, may overrule the alternative selected on monetary grounds.

Another value of the decision tree approach if it is used for numerical evaluation, is that probability estimates have to be made in numerical terms and these have to be supported by some evidence or logical argument.

In the various parts of the literature which discuss decision analysis and decision trees it is a fairly common view that these techniques are appropriate only to problems which are significant in terms of the company's resources. This may mean that many people who operate at a slightly lower 'decision level' may not bother exploring the subject because they feel it is not relevant.

It is of the utmost importance that both these misconceptions should be dispelled. The fact is that the decision tree technique is an economical and efficient tool to use even in relatively 'low

10

level' decision making. What is important is the recognition that the problem of whether to say install a coffee vending machine does not warrant six months market research and elaborate computer models; but the alternatives open—the possible events which can happen may be displayed in decision tree form. The probabilities of these events may be estimated by the decision maker on prior knowledge. Simple calculations will provide him with the choice he should make, given that he has estimated the financial outcomes.

Another important feature of this technique is that it can be used to explore beyond the present decision. This sequential decision making means that management take into account now the impact of decisions which may be made in the future. Hence the situation may arise where a particular alternative may be selected now or in two or three periods' time. Even if the absolute financial outcome were the same in both cases, the application of discounted cash flow analysis may indicate that the decision should be made now. The importance of these considerations lies in the ability to explicitly introduce 'timing' into the decision process.

To summarise the advantages of using the decision tree technique, the following benefits are achieved:

the structure of the problem is logically displayed

all realistic decision alternatives are shown

all relevant chance events, of any consequence, are detailed

the consequential outcome involved in each alternative act given that specific events occur is shown

sequential decision making is easily accommodated

all prior probabilities and costs of taking various courses of action are shown

each estimate, especially where it is critical, is supported by logical reasoning

the necessary numerical calculations can be performed on the same record sheet

other factors such as personal preference or risk acceptibility may be shown

it permits management to take account to a greater extent the impact on present decisions of possible future acts

incorporating the techniques of discounted cash flow enables the relative values of present and future profits to be taken into account.

DETAILED NUMERICAL EXAMPLE OF THE DECISION TREE TECHNIQUE

Since even a moderately complex business problem may require considerable calculation and information analysis, a relatively straightforward problem is considered here. Little reference is made to the ways in which probability estimates are formulated by the decision maker. The aim is to show how the decision tree technique provides the benefits described in the last section.

The problem is that of a private shareholder who owns 10,000 shares purchased a year previously at 60*s*. per share—total cost of £30,000. The share price exhibited fluctuations during the year roughly in line with the overall market. At the half-way stage, promising results reported by the company led to an increase in activity of the shares. At the end of September they stood at 80*s*. per share—a price which was high relative to the overall market movements. The shareholder thought that the price could be realistic if it accurately reflected good results by the company which would be reported at the end of the year.

He had always shown a strong interest in the affairs of the company and considered that he had a good idea of its potential. His view was that the current price may have been pushed too high but he also thought there was a 'fair' chance that the results at the end of the year would substantiate the present price, and even support a further increase.

From the information he had available, including advice from his stockbroker, and the various analyses he had carried out he was able to put his thoughts into quantitative form.

He thought there was a 30 per cent probability that the share price at the end of December would increase to 90*s*. However, he felt more strongly that the price could fall to 70*s*. and allocated a probability of 50 per cent to this event. This meant that there was a 20 per cent chance that the price would be static at 80s. and he agreed that this deduction was realistic.

To maintain simplicity, other values were omitted from the analysis. The inclusion of say 85s. and 75s. would only introduce more branches into the decision tree. It was assumed that dividend payments could be ignored in the first analysis but would be included in the later analyses, and hence this example does not consider dividends—again for simplicity. Again in the actual analysis, taxation was taken into account, but is omitted from the analysis shown here. Hence all financial outcomes are in gross terms.

Looking beyond the end of the year the shareholder considered that by the end of the following March the shares would

SHARE PRICE NOW (END OF SEPTEMBER)	SHARE PRICE AT END OF DECEMBER	SHARE PRICE AT END OF NEXT MARCH

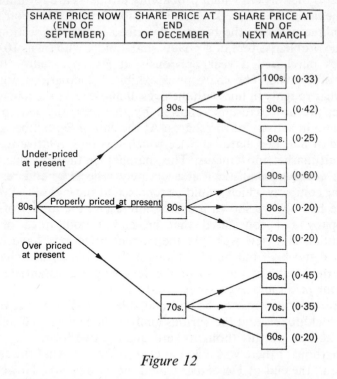

Figure 12

THE EVENT TIME PATH IN THE SHAREHOLDING PROBLEM

be priced between 60*s*. at the minimum, to 100*s*. at the maximum. He felt that if the present price failed to discount fully the company's future performance, then an increase to 90*s*. at the end of December could be followed by a further increase to 100*s*. by the end of March. Similarly, he felt that the market could over-value the shares at the end of the year and that the price might fall back to 80*s*. by the end of March.

If the shares were correctly valued now, then the price is likely to be 80*s*. at the end of the year and could move to 90*s*. by the end of March. However he felt that there was some chance that a fall to 70*s*. would occur.

Finally he considered that if the shares were currently over-valued then the price might fall to 70*s*. at the end of the year. If it did, then a further fall to 60*s*. by the end of March could not be ruled out. However, he felt that the new year could change the downward trend, if it occurred, and result in a price at the end of March of 80*s*.

Figure 12 shows the time path of the different events the shareholder thought might occur.

Having specified the events which he thought may occur, from all the various alternatives before him he selected the three which he thought to be the most realistic.

Alternative A: Retain complete holding
Alternative B: Sell complete holding
Alternative C: Sell half of his holding

The next step was to assign probability estimates to each of the second period events, that is share prices at the end of March. The probabilities allocated to each event are shown in *Table 3*. Since he was more familiar with gambling terminology —that is odds against,[1] this method was used to obtain the probability estimates. Both odds against and probabilities are shown in the table.

---

[1] Odds against is an expression often used by gamblers to express the probability of an event—for example if the probability of event A occurring is $p(A) = 0.4$, or 40 per cent, this implies that there are a total of, say, 100 outcomes of which 40 correspond with success and 60 correspond with failure. The ratio 60:40 or 3:2 represents the 'odds against it happening.' Alternatively if $p(A) = 0.4$ and $p(\overline{A}) = 1 - 0.4 = 0.6$ then odds against can be expressed as $p(A):p(A)$ or $0.6:0.4$ or 3:2.

Probabilities that share price will be at specific levels at the end of March

Table 3

Price at end of March	Probability	Odds against
100s.	0·10	9 to 1
90s.	0·25	3 to 1
80s.	0·35	2 to 1
70s.	0·20	4 to 1
60s.	0·10	9 to 1

He had already estimated the probability of the share price being at specific levels at the end of the year—that is 90s. $= 0·3$; 80s. $= 0·2$; 70s. $= 0·5$.

Clearly, if the price at the end of December were say 70s. then he would revise the probability estimate for the price being at 70s. at the end of March, from 0·2 to some figure above that value. To obtain these conditional probabilities the shareholder was told to imagine that it was now the end of December and that he now knew the price to be 90s. Then from his past knowledge and knowing this price he estimated probabilities for various price levels at the end of March. This process was repeated for each of the possible prices at the end of December. These conditional probabilities are shown in *Figure 12* in brackets.

Having specified the alternative choices of action and the different events which may occur, the decision tree can be drawn up. This is shown in *Figure 13* on pages 152–153. Each of the decisions that can be made now, can also be made at the end of the year. If the present decision is to retain half his holding and this is followed by a similar decision at the end of December then at the end of March, only ¼ of his present shares will be held—that is 2,500 shares.

Financial outcomes are calculated by multiplying the number of shares held at the end of March by the price at that terminal point. This is then divided by $(1·03)^2$ to obtain the present value—that is it is assumed that the shareholder can invest his capital to earn 3 per cent gross per quarter. If a sale of shares is made at the end of December then the number of shares multiplied by the price at that time, divided by 1·03 yields the present value. Similarly if shares are sold now, the present value is simply the number of shares sold multiplied by the present price. The total financial outcome, as shown on the decision tree, is the sum of these three sources of cash.

Figure 14 summarises these financial outcomes and the decisions and events which lead to them. This *figure* is in fact a tabular version of the decision tree and may be used if the latter is difficult to follow.

The analysis is carried out by multiplying the financial outcome shown in the decision tree by the relevant probability. The expected value of a specific second stage decision branch is therefore the sum of the expected values at its terminal points.

For example if the first and second stage decisions are to retain the holding then from either the decision tree or *Figure 14* on pages 154–155, the expected value of the later decision is the sum of

47,130 × 0·33 = 15,710	that is—present decision:retain holding
42,510 × 0·42 = 17,854	future event:share price to 90s.
37,700 × 0·25 = 9,425	future decision:retain holding

42,989

Similarly the expected value for the present decision to retain the holding followed by a later decision to sell half of his holding at 90s., is £43,393.

All the expected values for all future decisions are calculated and the one with the highest value is recorded on the decision tree. The other alternatives are then made redundant by marking with a \ . In the case of the decision now to retain holding and in the event of share price increasing to 90s. the highest expected value is £43,790 for case B—that is sell complete holding.

In the case where the share price is static at 80s., the best later decision choice is to retain half the holding at that time— that is expected value = £40,624.

In the third case where the share price falls to 70s. the best later decision would be to sell the complete holding at that time. The expected value of that course of action is £34,167.

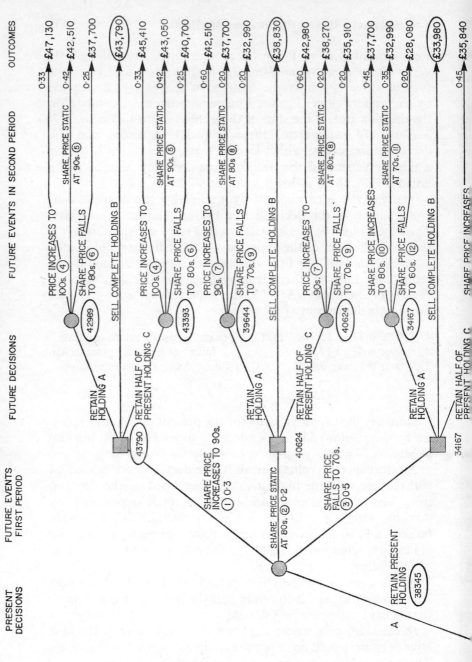

DECISION TREE DEPICTING PROBLEM OF DECIDING WHETHER TO RETAIN SHAREHOLDING

PRESENT DECISIONS | FUTURE EVENTS FIRST PERIOD | FUTURE DECISIONS | FUTURE EVENTS IN SECOND PERIOD | OUTCOMES

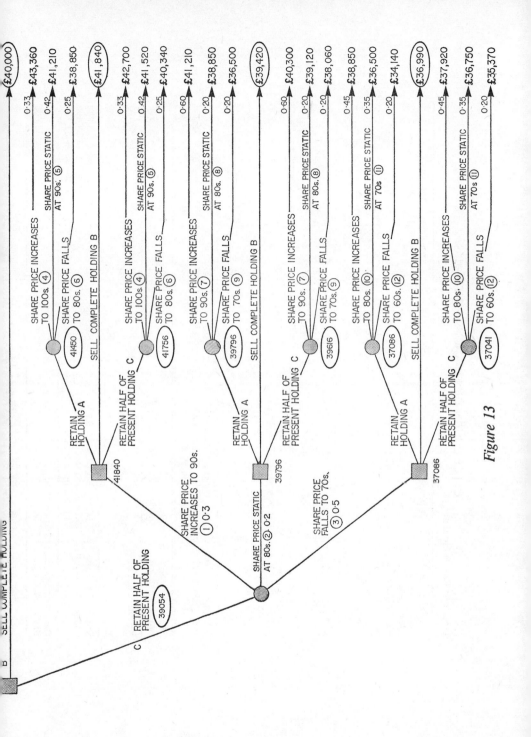

Figure 13

Decision: Retain Holding

CALCULATION OF FINANCIAL OUTCOMES

LATER ACTION	FINANCIAL OUTCOME (£)	EVENT	FINANCIAL OUTCOME (£)
Share price increases to 90s.			
Sell holding	$10,000 \times 4·5/1·03 = 43,790$		$= 43,790$
Retain holding		Price 100s.	$10,000 \times 5·0/(1·03)^2 = 47,130$
		,, 90s.	$10,000 \times 4·5/(1·03)^2 = 42,510$
		,, 80s.	$10,000 \times 4·0/(1·03)^2 = 37,700$
Sell half holding and retain the rest	$5,000 \times 4·5/1·03 = 21,840$ to be added to each of next financial outcomes.	100s.	$5,000 \times 5·0/(1·03)^2 + 21,840 = 45,410$
		,, 90s.	$5,000 \times 4·5/(1·03)^2 + 21,840 = 43,050$
		,, 80s.	$5,000 \times 4·0/(1·03)^2 + 21,840 = 40,700$
Share price static at 80s.			
Sell holding	$10,000 \times 4·0/1·03 = 38,830$		$= 38,830$
Retain holding		Price 90s.	$10,000 \times 4·5/(1·03)^2 = 42,510$
		,, 80s.	$10,000 \times 4·0/(1·03)^2 = 37,700$
		,, 70s.	$10,000 \times 3·5/(1·03)^2 = 32,990$
Sell half holding and retain the rest	$5,000 \times 4·0/1·03 = 19,420$ to be added to each of next financial outcomes.	80s.	$5,000 \times 4·5/(1·03)^2 + 19,420 = 42,980$
		,, 80s.	$5,000 \times 4·0/(1·03)^2 + 19,420 = 38,270$
		,, 70s.	$5,000 \times 3·5/(1·03)^2 + 19,420 = 35,910$
Share price declines to 70s.			
Sell holding	$10,000 \times 3·5/1·03 = 33,980$		$= 33,980$
Retain holding		Price 90s.	$10,000 \times 4·0/(1·03)^2 = 37,700$
		,, 70s.	$10,000 \times 3·5/(1·03)^2 = 32,990$
		,, 60s.	$10,000 \times 3·0/(1·03)^2 = 28,280$
Sell half holding and retain the rest	$5,000 \times 3·5/1·03 = 16,990$ to be added to each of next financial outcomes.	80s.	$5,000 \times 4·0/(1·03)^2 + 16,990 = 35,840$
		,, 70s.	$5,000 \times 3·5/(1·03)^2 + 16,990 = 33,490$
		,, 60s.	$5,000 \times 3·0/(1·03)^2 + 16,990 = 31,130$

Decision: Sell Complete Holding
10,000 shares at 80s. $= 40,000$

Figure 14

CALCULATION OF FINANCIAL OUTCOMES

Decision: Retain Half Present Holding

LATER ACTION	FINANCIAL OUTCOME (£)	EVENT	FINANCIAL OUTCOME (£)
Price increases to 90s.			
Sell holding	$20,000 + 5,000 \times 4·5/1·03 = 41,840$		$= 41,840$
Retain holding		Price 100s.	$20,000 + 5,000 \times 5·0/(1·03)^2 = 43,560$
		,, 90s.	$20,000 + 5,000 \times 4·5/(1·03)^2 = 41,210$
		,, 80s.	$20,000 + 5,000 \times 4·0/(1·03)^2 = 38,850$
Sell half holding and retain the rest	$20,000 + 2,500 \times 4·5/1·03 = 30,920$ to be added to each of next financial outcomes.	100s.	$30,920 + 2,500 \times 5·0/(1·03)^2 = 42,700$
		,, 90s.	$30,920 + 2,500 \times 4·5/(1·03)^2 = 41,520$
		,, 80s.	$30,920 + 2,500 \times 4·0/(1·03)^2 = 40,340$
Share price static at 80s.			
Sell holding	$20,000 + 5,000 \times 4·0/1·03 = 39,420$		$= 39,420$
Retain holding		Price 90s.	$20,000 + 5,000 \times 4·5/(1·03)^2 = 41,210$
		,, 80s.	$20,000 + 5,000 \times 4·0/(1·03)^2 = 38,850$
		,, 70s.	$20,000 + 5,000 \times 3·5/(1·03)^2 = 36,500$
Sell half holding and retain the rest	$20,000 + 2,500 \times 4·0/1·03 = 29,700$ to be added to each of next financial outcomes.	90s.	$29,700 + 2,500 \times 4·5/(1·03)^2 = 40,300$
		,, 80s.	$29,700 + 2,500 \times 4·0/(1·03)^2 = 39,120$
		,, 70s.'	$29,700 + 2,500 \times 3·5/(1·03)^2 = 38,060$
Share price falls to 70s.			
Sell holding	$20,000 + 5,000 \times 3·5/1·03 = 36,990$		$= 36,990$
Retain holding		Price 80s.	$20,000 + 5,000 \times 4·0/(1·03)^2 = 38,850$
		,, 70s.	$20,000 + 5,000 \times 3·5/(1·03)^2 = 36,500$
		,, 60s.	$20,000 + 5,000 \times 3·0/(1·03)^2 = 34,140$
Sell half holding and retain the rest	$20,000 + 2,500 \times 3·5/1·03 = 28,500$ to be added to each of next financial outcomes.	80s.	$28,500 + 2,500 \times 4·0/(1·03)^2 = 37,920$
		,, 70s.	$28,500 + 2,500 \times 3·5/(1·03)^2 = 36,750$
		,, 60s.	$28,500 + 2,500 \times 3·0/(1·03)^2 = 35,570$

In the same way the best later decisions are evaluated for the other present decision. The relevant expected values are ringed on the decision tree.

Having evaluated the largest expected value in each case, the same procedure is continued to evaluate the present decision.

For example for the present decision to retain full holding, its expected value is:

$$0.3 \times 43,790 = 13,137$$
$$0.2 \times 40,624 = 8,125$$
$$0.5 \times 34,167 = 17,083$$

$$\overline{38,345}$$

Both this alternative and that of selling half of the holding now, yield expected values less than the alternative to sell the complete holding—that is its expected value is £40,000.

Clearly, on monetary grounds the decision should be to sell the complete holding, now valued at £40,000. However, the shareholder to some extent identified himself with the company and he was rather loathe to sell his complete holding. The alternative of retaining half his present holding has an expected value of a little over £39,000 and hence this was his eventual decision. Although he did not choose the best course of action in financial terms, he still decided rationally, because he knew the approximate cost of his personal preference (£1,000) and he could afford to pay the premium.

In addition this alternative still allowed the possibility of making a total return of nearly £44,000 if all went well. The alternative chosen was also less risky than alternative A where there existed a chance of making a total return of as little as £28,000, which compared with the minimum under alternative C of £34,000.

References

'Bayesian classification procedures in analysing customer characteristics', P. E. Green, *Journal of Marketing Research*, 1, 1964

'Bayesian statistics', F. J. Anscombe, *American Statistician*, 15, 1961

'Bayesian statistical inference for psychological research', W. Edwards, H. Lindman and L. J. Savage, *Psychological Review*, 70, 1963

'Bayesian decision theory in pricing strategy', P. E. Green, *Journal of Marketing*, 27, 1963

Studies in Subjective Probability, H. E. Kyburg and H. E. Smokler, New York, Wiley, 1964

'Decision trees for decision making', J. F. Magee, *Harvard Business Review*, 42, 1964

Applied Statistical Decision Theory, H. Raiffa and R. Schlaifer, Harvard University, 1961

Probability and its Engineering Uses, Thornton C. Fry, Princeton, N.J., Van Nostrand, 1965

An Introduction to Probability Theory and its Applications, W. Feller, New York, Wiley, 1957

Elementary Probability, E. O. Thorp, London, Wiley, 1966

CHAPTER 7

Case Study 1—A Disinvestment Problem

THE GENESIS OF THE PROBLEMS

This chapter is concerned with providing a practical example of
a real business situation where the approach and some of the
techniques of the previous chapters were used. Although the use
of techniques is important, the emphasis is on the approach to
the problem and the attitude of the analyst. For reasons of
confidentiality the precise situation is not identified, nor is
numerical data used which could pinpoint the business.

The business was a relatively small division of a large company and its products were large-value capital goods sold mainly
in the United Kingdom. Its markets could be segmented into
four product areas and six industrial areas. Contracts were
obtained by preparing tenders and bidding against various
competitors, some of whom specialised in product markets and
some specialised in industrial segments. Although the division
had competed in some export markets in addition, the contracts
it had obtained tended to be unprofitable.

The main problem facing the division was that the level of
activity was falling off and hence it was failing to make an
acceptable return on capital employed. This shortcoming appeared to be on a long-term trend and there was no information to support the management's view that the historical
downward trend would be reversed in the near future.

It was thought that the cause of the underlying trend lay in a
decline in the total market available and consequent increase
in competition. This led to another view that a more systematic
and realistic pricing and bidding policy could bring about the
change required. The other causative factors were thought
to be the organisation of the management structure and

inadequate production facilities. Some efforts had already been made to improve the management team but the production difficulties would have been difficult to obviate without a major capital investment. Such an investment would not have been warranted in view of the small size and lack of growth of the total market.

Another possibility might have been to acquire one of the division's more successful competitors and combine the two businesses into one more powerful unit, but this would have required major capital investment and in addition a policy decision to expand considerably the company's interests in this market.

The whole exercise appeared to develop from a request by divisional management to 'get some information' about their market. This request, in fact, developed from central management's dissatisfaction with the progress the division was making. The divisional management knew that further market information was required but were unable to state precisely the nature of their requirements. This was probably due to their reluctance to face squarely the issues involved. In the past, improvements in both turnover and return on capital employed had been predicted and consistent failure to maintain targets was blamed on inadequate production facilities and unfair overhead allocation.

Although there was some truth in both the complaints, these were constraints, possibly permanent, on the business within which its management had to operate as efficiently as possible. If the most efficient operation which could be achieved under the existing constraints was still unacceptable then there would be grounds for closing the business. Management that had failed to optimise their resources in difficult conditions may very well fail to do so under better conditions. They may produce a better result if the constraints are removed but still far from the standard which could be reached.

One important criterion in financial terms is some specific return on capital employed and this is often applied by central management to the various businesses making up the corporation. It is arguable whether this sort of criterion is adequate even when supported by other 'blanket' criteria. There must be a criterion specifying some minimum requirement, but apart from such a minimum, there should be different sets of criteria for each different business. These may be comparisons with other companies in the same industry or may be based on theoretical financial considerations. An acceptable return is one that not only satisfies the minimum criterion but one which also compares favourably with what similar companies achieve. If control procedures are based on these wider criteria then not only is financial control properly exercised but the achievements of divisional management are also monitored.

In the case of the division in question its results failed to satisfy a criterion based on even a minimum requirement. Even so, there would be no real argument to support the claim that the business should be closed until a thorough examination had been made. The purpose of this examination would be to determine where the real weaknesses lay and whether the business could be turned into a viable concern. Thus there were several alternatives before central management apart from disinvestment.

THE FORMULATION OF THE PROBLEM

The possible choices of action before central management were as follows:

1. allow the business to continue its present operations;
2. make management changes and allow the business to continue;
3. make capital investment to increase production capacity and make production facilities more efficient;
4. acquire a successful competitor and combine the businesses into one larger and more viable concern;
5. sell the business as it stands;
6. seek ways of making it more competitive by introducing more efficient marketing policies;
7. expand the product range to take the business into new market segments;
8. running down the business and closing it;
9. closing down manufacture and continuing as design consultants;

10. various combinations of these alternatives possibly in a sequential manner.

These decision alternatives are examined in detail one by one later in the chapter.

The specific states of nature relevant to these decision alternatives were essentially as follows:

(*a*) the size and growth of the United Kingdom market broken down by market segment—including those areas where the division had not been operating;

(*b*) the performance of the division in each of these segments and how likely they were to improve or otherwise on past performance;

(*c*) the extent of competition and whether the growth and profit records of the major competitors compared favourably with that of the division;

(*d*) the potential future performance of these competitors;

(*e*) whether a changed management structure would have a beneficial effect;

(*f*) the size and growth of export markets and the level of profitability likely to be obtained by expanding overseas interests;

(*g*) whether any technological innovation would provide a long-term threat to the division's prospects;

(*h*) whether a market existed for design consultancy;

(*i*) whether any structural market change might occur which would increase competition or lower prices;

(*j*) the effect of foreign competitors entering the field.

The list of states was intended as a series of broad headings. For example in case (*a*) market demand could be poor, good or excellent in the first year and the following year differ from the first. Hence forecasts were required for demand for some considerable period ahead for each market segment. In addition profitability forecasts were also required.

The problem of course was to choose one alternative from the ten given. Suppose alternative (1) had been chosen and demand decreased substantially, then the effects of this reduction could have been measured in financial terms. Similarly if the market improved and the division gained a larger share the effects of this event on profits would have been estimable. The approach to the problem then was to ask the questions: 'What is the probability of event A occurring? If it does and I have already chosen alternative B, what effect will this have on my sales and profits?'

By working backwards from future events to future decisions and to future events and present decisions, from the calculated costs and probabilities involved a rational choice could be made.

Hence the problem became one of estimating the probabilities that various events would occur or fail to occur and assessing the effects of such occurrences on the choices which were to be made. Part of this problem was therefore dealt with by market research and other information gathering methods applicable to the external market. The remaining part of the problem was tackled by an historical analysis of the company's records especially those relating to sales and profits. Since it was thought that their pricing and bidding policy was inadequate a major part of this historical analysis was related to examining this question.

The main purpose of this case study is to consider the pricing and bidding investigation rather than the market research study. However, the two exercises are not completely separable and hence the research study will be considered. In fact the historical analysis commenced before the market research and in addition to laying the foundations to the pricing model which was subsequently formulated, also permitted the more precise formulation of the market research requirements. This was intentional. It is a common experience that an analysis of internal historical data will often permit a more efficient research study to be carried out.

Since the two approaches were proceeding simultaneously at some stages it would not be practicable to write this account in a strictly chronological order. However, the actual sequence of events is roughly the same.

FORMULATION OF THE NON-MATHEMATICAL MODEL

The first step in the exercise was to obtain the necessary data.

The data required consisted of details of all contracts for which the division had submitted tenders over the past five years. The precise requirements were as follows:

the date the enquiry was received;

the date the tender was submitted;

whether or not additional tenders for a specific contract were submitted by the division;

whether the tender was successful or not and the date the order was placed, if relevant;

the total value of the contract;

a detailed description of the specification—that is, how many units and their dimensions;

how many competitors submitted competing bids;

the names of these competitors if possible;

in the case of an unsuccessful bid by the division, the name of the competitor who succeeded;

the main reasons why the competitor succeeded—that is, price, delivery, technical performance or other factors;

the name of the customer;

whether the customer had placed an order with the division before;

the industrial classification of the customer;

any special circumstances which affected a specific tender.

There were basic records available which gave considerable detailed information but in a form which was extremely difficult to extract. The possibility of using a computer for the classification was considered but rejected on the grounds that it would take as long as a manual approach and cost several times as much. Hence the information was extracted manually. In fact there were considerable advantages in doing it this way, not the least of which was that in some cases the information was either contradictory or missing. As these questions arose a brief conversation with one of the salesmen or the marketing manager usually provided the answer.

Each contract in each six month period was first classified by whether the division was successful or not. These were then grouped within the above classification by product segment and cross-classified by industrial sector and within these further classifications arranged into a size distribution. The size distribution was by contract value and by numbers of units.

From these classifications an attempt was made to estimate the probability of the division being successful when bidding in a specific product/industrial segment for a contract within a specific size range.

The first point that emerged was that the division appeared to have had an increasing probability of success as the contract value increased. This applied to certain segments but not to all. In one segment the division had obtained every large value contract for which it had bid. In another segment it had secured only one success in five years although a considerable number of tenders had been submitted.

The next classification was made by sorting the successful contracts into size order (by value) and cross-classifying by numbers of units and technical specifications, the latter being roughly defined by two physical measurements. There was very strong evidence to suggest that the unit value was highly related to the technical specification, in a way that could be measured.

Further classifications involved the unsuccessful tenders. These were grouped as before and cross-classified by the competitor which was successful and as far as was known, the reasons for his success, price, and quoted delivery period. In most cases the relevant prices were known. One piece of missing information was the technical specification of the tender submitted by the competitor. Since it was impossible to obtain this, the term 'value equivalent' was coined. This meant that if the division had quoted for say 2 units of specific dimensions then the contract was supposed to be for units equivalent to those two. The rare cases where the contract was lost for reasons other than price or delivery could not be classified as this usually meant that the order was obtained by the competitor on technical grounds. In other words, the specification submitted by the division was not applicable or acceptable. These cases were omitted.

From the various classifications and their graphical representation several hypotheses were formulated. Some of these were as follows:

the division has a higher probability of success when bidding for work in specific product/industrial segments and a very low probability of success in one or two others;

the division's probability of success increases sharply as the contract value increases, with the exception of one specific sector;

the value of the units appeared to be highly correlated with two specific dimensions which roughly determined the specification of the units;

certain competitors appeared to be strong in some sectors and almost absent in others;

the principal criterion which was used by the customer in deciding to whom to give the contract was price; only in one or two cases was it on delivery or technical grounds. This is presumably because the leading companies in this field were roughly as technically competent as one another and the delivery period would be of almost no consequence against price and technical performance. In any event, since the division generally operated at a level of production somewhat below its capacity, it was unlikely to lose an order for this reason.

Although various approaches were tried or considered, eventually it was concluded that a model might be obtainable from the technical data. This model would be used to predict the expected market value for a given type of product and would assign a probability distribution to these predictions which would describe the occurrence of values differing from the expected values by specific amounts.

These probabilities, derived from regression equations could then be revised according to criteria based on empirical evidence as soon as further information became available. Hence it was argued that a regression equation would be obtained, relating these two dimensions to unit market value, and would be used to predict the value that the market would set on a contract of a specific type. The expected market value so calculated would have an associated probability distribution which would be used to assess the probability of the division being successful given that it submitted a tender at a particular price.

However a model that finished at that stage would be inadequate since it failed to take into account any of the following factors:

differing number of competitors for a given contract;

reputation of the competitors against whom the division was bidding;

the usual case where the contract consisted of several units of perhaps differing size;

special technical or commercial considerations relevant to that particular case only;

customer's preferences and prejudices.

It was argued that the first deficiency could be overcome by assuming that the model was based on an average number of competitors in the past and specifying this number. Having made this assumption it followed that if in a particular case the number of competitors was known to be above this average number then the division's probability of success would be decreased. Similarly if it were found that less than the average number were competing then the probability of success would be adjusted upwards. These effects could be handled in a simple way by assuming that each competitor had an equal chance of succeeding and using the addition law of probability.

The average number of competitors in the past had been three. When the division bid for a specific contract at a price

which the model indicated it gave a probability of being successful of 20 per cent, then this implied that the probability of losing
the order was 80 per cent. It therefore followed that the
probability of at least one of the three competitors submitting
a lower and hence successful bid was also 80 per cent. From
this, the probability of each competitor being successful,
assuming each to have an equal chance, could be calculated by
using the addition law of probability.

Suppose the probability of success of each of the three
competitors is represented by $p(A)$, then the probability that
at least one is successful is given by the formula:

$$3 p(A) - 3 [p(A)]^2 + [p(A)]^3$$

and this expression equals 80 per cent. Therefore,

$$3 p(A) - 3 [p(A)]^2 + [p(A)]^3 = 0.8$$

must be solved for $p(A)$.

The only assumption was that each competitor was considered to have an equal chance of success, and in the above
case the solution of the equation yielded the probability of
$p(A)$ as 40 per cent.

Suppose that divisional market intelligence had found out in a
particular case that seven competitors were in fact bidding, then
assuming that each had the same probability of success as
above—that is 40 per cent, then the revised probability of the
division being successful could be calculated. This only required
that the probability of at least one of the seven being successful
was calculated.

This probability is calculated from the following expression:

$$1 - [1 - p(A)]^7 \text{ or } 1 - [1 - 0.4]^7$$

and hence the probability that the division was successful under
these circumstances was:

$$1 - 1 - [1 - p(A)]^7 = (1 - 0.4)^7 = 0.047$$

The model was used to calculate the division's prior probability of success when bidding at a specific value. When
further information was received this permitted the probability
to be revised. The calculation of the initial probability depended upon the assumption that all competitors had equal
probabilities of success. However, it was known from the
original classification exercise that certain competitors had
higher probabilities of success when bidding for a particular

type of contract. Hence if some approximate measure of the increased, or decreased, probability were made of each competitor this could be incorporated into the model.

Suppose further information concerning a specific contract became available—that of the seven competitors, three had been particularly unsuccessful in the past for this type of work, three had been average, or perhaps could not be identified, and one had been exceptionally successful in the past. Then the division's probability of success would be revised yet again to take this information into account. Reverting to the addition law of probability, instead of allocating an equal probability to each competitor, their individual probabilities were adjusted according to the prior knowledge of their historical performance or of the marketing manager's current assessment of their capabilities. This was extremely important as it permitted the use of current information, in the evaluation of the prospects for a given contract. For example the marketing manager would have used his knowledge of the prevailing market conditions to formulate his own subjective probability estimate and incorporate this into the model.

Where a contract was for several different sized units, the expected value of the contract was the sum of the expected values of the separate units. The probability distribution for the contract value was derived from the separate distributions of each unit. The principle remains unaltered except that the contract size might in itself have reduced the probability of success of some competitors, for example the smaller businesses. This however, was again relatively easy to deal with.

Special technical or commercial factors could only have been dealt with at the time of considering whether to tender or not and expert judgements of the situations would have been made. Again these could have been dealt with in the form of personal probability estimates and incorporated into the model to calculate revised probabilities of success.

THE GENERATION OF INFORMATION REQUIREMENTS

The specification of the problem in the form of decision

alternatives and occurrence of events, led to requirements for information to allow the probability of each event occurring to be estimated. In addition, the financial implications of the various alternatives needed to be assessed. Some of this information was obtainable from within the organisation, and some of it was obtained from the market survey.

The formulation of the pricing and bidding exercise into the form described on pages 165-8, generated further information requirements. These related to the analysis and mathematical development of the model and data to test its effectiveness. In addition, information would be required if the model were applied to the practical situation. For example, if the marketing manager were to revise the prior probabilities of success derived from the model when a specific price level was considered, then some form of market intelligence system must be established to provide a continuous flow of up-to-date information.

The information requirements for the development of the model were discussed on pages 163-4. However, the internal records held only limited data. Not much was known about the main competitors and insufficient was known about the external market—that is the extent to which demand was growing or decreasing or whether competition was increasing or not. Further, more information was required on the buying influences acting on the customers and of any likely industrial rationalisation, the occurrence of which might result in changed market parameters. This was important since the market parameters would be either explicitly or implicitly incorporated into the model.

Another point was that if the division adopted a more systematic approach to bidding and became more successful at winning orders, then a competitive reaction could occur. If information could be obtained to allow some assessment of the extent to which such a reaction could happen, then it would be worthwhile investigating.

Since a market survey was in the course of being organised it was a relatively simple matter to incorporate some of these questions into the questionnaire part of the survey. The market survey was designed to include a series of personal interviews and it was hoped that some of the more subjective questions could be handled at this level.

Certainly, the survey presented a good opportunity to gather information to help in the estimation of prior probabilities required for use by the model as demonstrated by *Figure 15*.

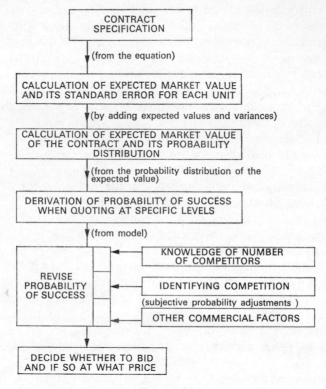

Figure 15

FORMULATION AND REVISION OF PRIOR PROBABILITIES

The proper time for prior probabilities to be revised is at the time of deciding for a particular contract, whether or not to bid and at what level. Hence the need for a system to provide a continuous flow of information.

The object of having such an information system was to

build up a more comprehensive picture of the market structure so that the marketing manager could use all available information in revising the prior probabilities of success.

Providing the model was efficient it could be used as a basis for the division's overall marketing and production strategy. For example, pricing decisions could be based upon the amount of work required to absorb production capacity. If the capacity were fully used then the quantity of work required could be calculated. From an approximate knowledge of the contracts which will arise during an oncoming year it would be possible to calculate the prices which would have to be quoted if there were to be a high probability of obtaining sufficient work. From these prices it would be possible to calculate whether acceptable margins would be made.

If such a pricing policy were used it would be as a yardstick. If orders were building up too rapidly and production capacity was approaching saturation then prices might be adjusted to decrease the probability of success. The reverse would be the case where the division was unable to obtain sufficient orders and hence were compelled to be satisfied with a low profit level—or alternatively, compelled to cut back on capacity.

The great advantage of using a formal model to attempt to deal with part of these complex problems is that it encourages a systematic approach. It is likely to result in clearer internal information systems being formed because the decision maker will see more clearly what information he needs. Even if the basic model is only an approximate representation of reality, its importance is as much in allowing the decision maker to see his problems earlier and more lucidly as for evaluation. However good the model is the decision maker almost inevitably has to use current market information to adjust the original probability estimates. These adjustments may finish up a long way from the original prior probabilities.

FORMULATION OF THE PREDICTING EQUATIONS

The typical contract was for a number of units each of which was specified by its length and diameter. It was found that the price of a unit varied closely with changes in these two dimensions and further that this causal relationship could be represented by an equation.

If P_k represents the price of a unit having a length X_k and diameter Y_k then the equation used can be written down as

$$P_k = a + bX_k + c \log Y_k$$

where a, b and c are constants. Hence for a given value of X and a given value of Y it was possible to estimate the expected market value for the unit by substituting these in the equation.

The next step was to calculate the probability distribution of the expected price calculated from the equation, for a given unit. This distribution denoted $p(X_k, Y_k)$ for a given unit was used to estimate the probability that the division would succeed if it tendered at a specific price.

In the case where the contract was for more than one unit, the expected contract value was equal to the sum of the unit prices. The variance of the contract price was assumed equal to the sum of the variances of the individual units and hence the standard error of the contract price was obtained by calculating the positive square root of the variance.

The next step was to take into account current market information on the numbers and identities of competitors, and use this information to revise the prior probabilities.

Figure 15 on page 170 demonstrates the way in which the prior probabilities derived from the model are subsequently revised to utilise latest information.

Instead of describing the actual formulation used in further detail, a numerical example is given to show how the relationship, if any, between two variables may be approximately established by regression methods. A linear form is considered and the way in which the probability distribution of the estimate is derived is also shown. This example is developed into a simple version of the pricing and bidding model, for simplicity.

If the price of the kth unit is P_k and its main dimension is X_k, then it is required to find a linear relationship of the form

$$P_k = a + bX_k$$

using the following data, which is displayed in *Figure 16*.

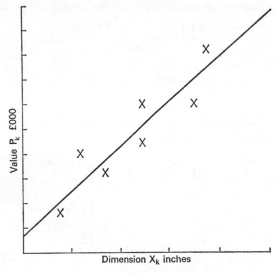

Figure 16

RELATIONSHIP BETWEEN PRICE OF EACH UNIT (£000)
AND ITS RADIUS (x INCHES)

Value P_k £000	Dimension X_k, inches
4·6	15
5·5	18
6·6	21
7·0	22
8·5	24
9·8	32

From the graphical representation the two variables appear to be linearly related and hence a straight line may be fitted to the observed data. This straight line may be used as the best estimate of the real relationship in the population of all pairs of observations of the two variables. For values beyond the sample range care should be taken.

A straightforward procedure for using the least squares criterion to estimate the parameters of the straight line—that is a and b in the equation $P = a + bX$—is as follows.

1. Calculate the mean of each of the above series—that is

$$\bar{X} = \frac{15 \text{ in} + \ldots + 32 \text{ in}}{6} = 22 \text{ in.}$$

and $\bar{P} = \frac{4 \cdot 6 + \ldots + 9 \cdot 8}{6} = 7$

2. These mean values are then subtracted from each value in the appropriate series as follows:

$p_k = P_k - \bar{P}$	$x_k = X_k - \bar{X}$
$4 \cdot 6 - 7 = -2 \cdot 4$	$15 - 22 = -7$
$5 \cdot 5 - 7 = -1 \cdot 5$	$18 - 22 = -4$
$6 \cdot 6 - 7 = -0 \cdot 4$	$21 - 22 = -1$
$7 \cdot 0 - 7 = 0 \cdot 0$	$22 - 22 = 0$
$8 \cdot 5 - 7 = 1 \cdot 5$	$24 - 22 = 2$
$9 \cdot 8 - 7 = 2 \cdot 8$	$32 - 22 = 10$

Each of the new values is termed x_k and p_k respectively to distinguish them from the previous values, X_k and Y_k.

3. Then multiply each of the xs by the corresponding ps and add together all such pairs:

$$(-7) \times (-2 \cdot 4) + (-4) \times (-1 \cdot 5) + (-1) \times (-0 \cdot 4) +$$
$$2 \times 1 \cdot 5 + 10 \times 2 \cdot 8 = 16 \cdot 8 + 6 + 0 \cdot 4 + 3 + 28 = 54 \cdot 2$$

This is termed the sum of the cross-products and is denoted by

$$\sum_{k=1}^{6} x_k p_k$$

4. The next step is to calculate the 'sum of the squares' of the xs, that is

$$(-7)^2 + (-4)^2 + (-1)^2 + (2)^2 + (10)^2 =$$
$$49 + 16 + 1 + 4 + 100 = 170$$

This is denoted by

$$\sum_{k=1}^{6} x_k^2$$

5. The sum of the cross-products is then divided by the sum of the squares,

$$\sum_{k=1}^{6} x_k p_k \ \bigg/ \ \sum_{k=1}^{6} x_k{}^2 = \frac{54\cdot2}{170} = 0\cdot319 \text{ units.}$$

This is the 'least squares' estimate of the slope of the line—that is the b coefficient.

6. The constant a which represents the intercept and specifies the position of the line is calculated from the b coefficient and the means of the Xs and the mean of the Ps as follows:

$$a = \bar{P} - b\bar{X} = 7 - 22 \times 0\cdot319 = -0\cdot02 \text{ units.}$$

The required equation can now be written

$$\bar{P}_k = 0\cdot02 + 0\cdot319\, X_k$$

Hence for a given value of X, the expected price may be calculated. For example if the unit had a 40 in radius then substituting this in the equation yields the required estimate of the price, that is

$$\begin{aligned}
\hat{P}_{x-40} &= -0\cdot02 + 0\cdot319 \times 40 \\
&= -0\cdot02 + 12\cdot76 \\
&= \qquad 12\cdot74
\end{aligned}$$

that is £12,740

The value £12,740 is the expected price of the unit. If the actual price were £12,000 or £13,000 this would cause no great surprise to the marketing manager because the expected value is the 'central value' and values close to it can easily occur. To proceed further it is necessary to establish a measure of the variation around this central value which would occur if say several hundred contracts for this size unit were to occur.

The required measure is called the standard error of estimate and for this specific case it can be calculated from the following formula

$$\text{Standard error} = \sqrt{\frac{\Sigma(\hat{P}_k - P_k)^2}{N(N-2)}} \left[1 + N + \frac{N(x_j)^2}{\Sigma x_k{}^2}\right]$$

The first part of this equation measures how well the calculated line fits the data. $\Sigma(\bar{P}_k - P_k)^2$ is the sum of the squares of the differences between the observed values and those calculated from the equation.

If these pairs are denoted P_1 to P_6 and X_1 to X_6 then the expected values are calculated by substituting each of the Xs in the equation

$$\hat{P} = -0.02 + 0.319X$$

These are as shown below:

$$P_1 = 4.6; \hat{P}_1 = 4.8 \text{ for } X_1 = 15 \text{ in}$$
$$P_2 = 5.5; \hat{P}_2 = 5.7 \text{ for } X_2 = 18 \text{ in}$$
$$P_3 = 6.6; \hat{P}_3 = 6.7 \text{ for } X_3 = 21 \text{ in}$$
$$P_4 = 7.0; \hat{P}_4 = 7.0 \text{ for } X_4 = 22 \text{ in}$$
$$P_5 = 8.5; \hat{P}_5 = 7.6 \text{ for } X_5 = 24 \text{ in}$$
$$P_6 = 9.8; \hat{P}_6 = 10.2 \text{ for } X_6 = 15 \text{ in}$$

as an example of how these are calculated, for $X_1 = 15$ in

$$\hat{Y}_1 = -0.02 + 0.319 \times 15$$
$$= -0.02 + 4.78$$
$$= \quad 4.8$$

From the above values of P_k and $\hat{P}_k$

$$\Sigma(\hat{P}_k - P_k)^2$$
$$= (4.8 - 4.6)^2 + (5.7 - 5.5)^2 + \ldots + (10.2 - 9.8)^2$$
$$= 0.04 + 0.04 + 0.01 + 0 + 0.81 + 0.16 = 1.06$$

Hence from the standard error equation the standard error of estimate for $\hat{Y}_2$ from $X_2 = 18$ inches is

$$\sqrt{\left[\frac{1.06}{N(N-2)}\right] \left[1 + N + N\frac{(18-22)^2}{170}\right]}$$
$$= \sqrt{\frac{1.06}{6 \times 4}} \left[1 + 6 + \frac{6 \times 16}{170}\right] \approx £580$$

If it is assumed that the probability distribution of the estimate is bell-shaped and approximately normal, then for $X = 18$ in the expected price is £5,700 and the range of values which cuts off 95 per cent of the distribution is approximately £5,700 ± £1,200 or from £4,500 to £6,900.

Figure 17, illustrates the expected market value as calculated and its probability distribution.

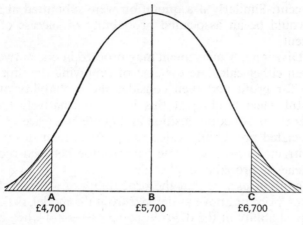

Figure 17

THE PROBABILITY DISTRIBUTION OF THE EXPECTED
MARKET UNIT VALUE

The value at A is the value which is 98% likely to be less than the
market value. The value at B is the units expected value. The value
at C is the value which is only likely to be exceeded with a probability
of about 00%.

THE DERIVATION OF THE PROBABILITY OF SUCCESS WHEN
QUOTING AT A GIVEN LEVEL

Suppose tenders were requested for a contract for one unit of
size 18 in then, if the division quoted at the expected value as
calculated in the last section that is £5,700, the probability of
being successful would be 50 per cent. This is because the model
is based on the values of successful bids in the past and hence
the expected values calculated correspond with the expected
market value for a unit of that size. Therefore the probability
distribution of the expected market value corresponds with the
probability of success. If the division quoted a price of £4,500
then from the calculated probability distribution of the
expected market value it is seen that there is approximately a
2 per cent chance that a lower quotation will occur. Hence the
division's probability of success in this case would be about

98 per cent. Similarly if a quotation were submitted at £6,900, there would be an associated probability of success of about 2 per cent.

The Divisional Management may proceed in one of two ways. They can either calculate the cost of supplying the unit plus a margin for profit and then consider the probability of being successful when bidding at this level. Alternatively they can consider the production position and quote at a price which has an associated probability value that reflects their desire to get the contract. In practice some compromise between these two approaches is probably applicable.

The concept used is that the probability of a contract going at a given price or above as derived from the model, is the same as the probability of the division being successful when bidding at this level.

From a comparison of the division's past performance against the values predicted by the model several points emerged. One was that in a particular segment the division consistently bid at values considerably above the expected market value. In one case their bid was 130 per cent higher than the successful bid if the data were to be believed. This corresponded with a probability of something like one chance in several hundred thousand of being successful. It was therefore not surprising that only one contract had been won in this segment during the past five years. Hence an immediate recommendation was to cease bidding for this type of contract if prices could not be considerably reduced. The actual cost of tendering could in some cases be considerable. Although no detailed cost information appeared to be available it was quite obvious that several thousand pounds could have been saved by more selective tendering. Also, the staff used for abortive tendering could have been better employed on contracts where the probability of success was higher.

In addition there were market areas where the division had been practically 100 per cent successful. It is possible that contracts in these segments were relatively insensitive to price and that the division could have put in higher value bids in some cases. Certainly in the cases where the division had a distinct design advantage this could be the case.

The view formed on the basis of the analysis was that if the division adopted a more selective and systematic approach to bidding it could improve its performance. The improvement might just be sufficient to earn an acceptable return on the resources used although it was strictly dependent upon the outside market. If the market research study found that demand was static or decreasing in segments important to the division then adopting a more rigorous approach to pricing and bidding would still not enable an acceptable return to be earned.

The original decision therefore depended upon the outcome of the research programme. However, such progress had been made with the pricing and bidding model that it was decided that it was worthwhile completing the model. It was recognised at the time that if the final decision were to close the division the model would never be used for pricing and bidding. However, if the demand factors were found to be satisfactory by the market research programme then there would be a ready-made pricing and bidding strategy for the divisional management to operate.

THE REVISIONS OF PRIOR PROBABILITIES ON THE BASIS OF LATEST INFORMATION

The linear predicting equation permits estimates to be made of the expected value of the contract given that it was for one unit of a specific dimension. The probability of the division being successful could be derived from it if a bid were made at a particular level.

If the model were to be anywhere near reality it must include or be capable of including the factors already mentioned and summarised below:

the model must be capable of dealing with contracts which consist of more than one unit and of different sizes;

it must be capable of incorporating information relating to the numbers of competitors known to be bidding in a particular case;

if further information became available on the names of the

actual competitors then in so far as some are more likely to succeed in a particular case than others, this knowledge needs to be incorporated into the model;

similarly if any special technical or commercial information was obtained, the probabilities specified by the model would require adjustment in the light of this information;

knowledge of customers preferences and prejudices would also be used, where an historical analysis provided useful information.

The problem of dealing with contracts for more than one unit was dealt with relatively easily. For example, one specific contract was for two 15 in units, one 21 in and three 24 in units the expected prices of which, as calculated on page 176 were £4,800, £6,700 and £7,600 per unit respectively.

Hence the expected value of the total contract was
$$2 \times £4,800 + 1 \times £6,700 + 3 \times £7,600 = £39,000.$$

Page 176 shows that the standard error for the 18 in units was calculated as £580. The standard errors calculated in the same way for the 15, 21 and 24 in units were found to be approximately £620, £560 and £560 respectively.

Each of the 15in units will have a standard error of £620 and similarly each of the 24 in units will have one of £560. The standard error of the total contract is calculated as follows
$$\sqrt{((2)^2 \times (620)^2 + (560)^2 + (3)^2 \times (560)^2)} \approx £2,200$$

This implies that the price of one unit is independent of the other units in the contract, which is probably untrue. However it serves as a reasonable approximation to reality.

Having calculated the expected contract value at £39,100 the standard error of £2,200 permits the estimation of the probability of success when bidding at say £38,000. This is exactly the same as shown in the previous section.

The way in which information on the number of competitors bidding is incorporated has already been described. The model was based on data which related to contracts where there were on average three other competitors bidding. The range of numbers could vary between zero and possibly ten in rare cases.

If the division intended to quote a price of say £38,000 which yielded, from the model, a probability of success of 40 per cent then when exactly three competitors were involved this prior probability would remain unchanged. If it were learnt that no competitors were bidding then clearly the division would be almost certain of getting the order and hence they may be advised to put in a higher price.

For any number of competitors other than zero or three, the average in the past, the revised probability of success is calculated by using the addition law of probability as explained in pages 135–6.

Note on computation on probabilities

To facilitate the computations, several tables and charts were prepared. The first consisted of a table classified by size of unit and cross-classified by the second dimension. In the cell the expected value was shown of a unit of these dimensions. Also shown was the square of its standard error—that is its variance.

All that was necessary, therefore, was to add the appropriate expected values and similarly add their variances and take the square root of the latter.

The next chart plotted the cumulative normal function, as shown in *Figure 18* on page 182, with the probabilities ranging from 1 to zero on the vertical axis. The horizontal axis was divided into grids as is shown ranging from -3 to $+3$ in steps of $\frac{1}{4}$. To use this it is necessary to subtract the value which the division proposes to submit from the expected contract value and call this new value d; and divide d by the calculated standard error. Unless an absurd value is proposed the result will lie between -3 and $+3$.

From the chart it is seen that $+3$ corresponds with almost certain failure while -3 corresponds with almost certain success. Zero on this scale corresponds with the expected market value, yielding a probability of success of 0·5.

This chart can be used for evaluating the probability of an event in any such problem where the distribution is approximately normal, providing the mean and standard deviation are known, or can be estimated.

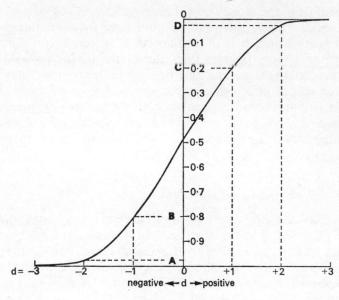

Figure 18

GRAPHICAL REPRESENTATION OF PROBABILITY OF SUCCESS
WHEN BIDDING AT VARIOUS LEVELS

The vertical axis is probability of success ranging from 1 to zero.
The horizontal scale is $d =$ [contract value − expected contract
value]/(standard error). Note in example where expected market
value = £39,100 and s.e. = £2,200. If a price of £34,700 is considered
then $d = (34,700 − 39,100)/2,200 = −2$
From the above curve, the value −2 is associated with a probability
of about 98 % (i.e. probability of success).

The third chart which was prepared for divisional management showed prior probabilities on the vertical scale. The
horizontal scale was graduated from zero to 10 corresponding
with the varying number of competitors. The cell entries were
revised prior probabilities—their values diminishing from 1—
that is certainty—in the first column to near zero in the last
column.

Hence all the decision maker had to do, once he had calculated the prior probability—that is read it off the first table,

and found out how many competitors were bidding, was to look in the appropriate column for the revised probability of success.

Dealing with knowledge of the identities of the competitors, or other commercial and technical information relevant to that specific case, was left to the marketing manager who adjusted the probabilities so far obtained as he saw fit. He could use the addition law of probability to include the identities of the different competitors. Beyond this he would have to use his knowledge of current market conditions to make adjustments. Hence no further charts were prepared.

The model and the charts helped to remove much of the uncertainty and to deal with pricing decision making in a more systematic manner.

ASSESSING MARKET DEMAND PATTERNS

The survey was carried out by sending postal questionnaires to two large user segments backed up by personal interviews, and covering the remaining segments by interviews. In addition the little published data then available was analysed.

The principal finding was that the overall market applicable to the division was growing at a reasonable rate, but that demand in one of the segments where the division was especially strong was declining rapidly and would continue to be low for several years ahead. In addition, a continental competitor was found to have entered the market within the past two years with an alternative design and this competitor appeared to be gaining ground rapidly.

The principal United Kingdom competitors exhibited varying degrees of growth and profitability and there appeared to be major industrial mergers pending. There was no unattached competitor who was sufficiently attractive to warrant considering acquisition. However, brief studies were carried out on the most likely candidates.

From the forecasts made, based on the survey results, it appeared that the division was unlikely to fully use existing capacity for the next five years and hence any capital investment programme to expand production was likely to have seriously adverse consequences, in terms of the division's return on capital employed.

Although the survey was aimed specifically at the segments in which the division operated it was necessary to form a view of the prospects in other segments. A summary of this view was that in these segments competition was very strong and in some cases the division had neither the necessary skills nor production facilities to enter these markets.

Considerable numerical data was obtained and this permitted a reasonably precise estimate of the current market to be made. By asking users, who were mainly local councils, to record their past installations it was possible to build up a good picture of the long-term trends. This was used to forecast future demand together with the users replies of their future likely requirements over the next five years. The amount of the total market available to the division was calculated by allowing for trends in market shares amongst the leading suppliers and taking into account the considerable gains made by the continental competitor.

SELECTING THE DECISION ALTERNATIVE

From the demand study, forecasts of total market demand for a period of five years ahead were made. The analysis of the level of profitability in the industry permitted estimates of future industry profit levels to be made.

Within these industrial forecasts, predictions were made for both sales and profits for five years ahead for the division. These basic forecasts were on the assumption that no structural changes occurred. Consideration was then given to sales and profit levels that might be achieved if the division became more efficient in one way or another.

The decision alternatives already listed on page 160 are now dealt with one by one in detail.

1. *Allow the business to continue its present operations*

It was established that the external environment was becoming increasingly unfavourable and from the forecasts of demand it was possible to estimate the likely future levels of sales given that no action was taken at present. From these sales forecasts profit forecasts were made and future cash flows derived. The expected present value of the future profits, discounted at the company's average cost of capital, were insufficient to support the decision to allow the continuance of the existing capital investment in the business. Even the future profits, at 10 per cent probability level, when discounted would not support the ordinary future financial requirements of the business. Hence this decision alternative was really redundant—simply because closure of the business would produce a far more favourable outcome. This particular alternative is often considered to be the same as 'indecision' on the part of the decision maker—that is not making a decision. Even if it is actually 'indecision' in a specific case the outcome is the same as a conscious decision to make no change.

It was considered that deciding to continue present operations but allowing for other future decisions was not very realistic in this case. Hence such sequential alternatives were not considered in any detail.

2. *Make management changes and allow the business to continue in its present form*

The cost of introducing such changes could be approximately estimated. The difficulty was in estimating the likely effect such a change may have. In view of the market environment it was thought that a change was unlikely to improve the return by more than 20 per cent. Hence in the calculations, future profits, as forecast previously, were increased so that within three years they were 20 per cent above the original predictions. Following a similar argument to the first case the present value of the expected future profits was still not acceptable—although it provided a better alternative than the first.

3. *Make capital investment to increase production capacity and make production facilities more efficient*

Since there was a low probability that market demand would

increase sufficiently to use the new capacity, any expansion would have to be at the expense of competitors' market shares. It was learnt that a move was afoot to merge some of the competitors into more viable groups and therefore it was likely that competition would increase. It was felt that such an investment programme at best would improve profits by the 20 per cent level considered under alternative (2). A similar calculation was made, on the basis of estimated costs of the necessary re-equipping programme and the amended profit forecasts. Again this did not seem to have a very high probability of resulting in an acceptable return. In addition there was a fairly high risk that adopting this alternative could substantially worsen the situation, in terms of return on capital employed.

4. *Acquire a successful competitor and combine the business into one large more viable concern*

From the market study it was found that some competitors were already discussing merger plans and these were at an advanced stage. The competitors involved in discussions were the only independent businesses—the remainder were part of larger organisations. None of the independent companies appeared to be very profitable and few appeared to be growing. In addition there were far better arguments for product and production rationalisation between them rather than between one or more of them and the division. This was mainly because the independent competitors tended to be much smaller companies who operated at the lower value end of the markets.

Hence an acquisition would almost inevitably require a decision to enter market segments where historically the division was weak. Since demand in these segments was also static it was unlikely that an acquisition would improve the division's performance. There would be little or no synergistic benefits. This in turn meant that such an acquisition should be judged solely on the performance of the acquisition candidate and not on rationalisation benefits. There were no candidates which exhibited an acceptable performance which was hardly surprising in an environment such as this.

5. *Sell the business as it stands*

This decision alternative was made redundant at a very early stage simply because the production facilities were enmeshed in a large business. The division could not be regarded as being an independent manufacturing organisation.

6. *Seek ways of making it more competitive by introducing more efficient marketing policies*

The main opportunity here appeared to be in the area of pricing and bidding. The construction of the model described earlier enabled rough estimates to be made of how far performance could have been improved in the past had the model been used, on the assumption that the model was reasonably representative and did not result in a severe market reaction.

From the analysis it appeared that performance in the past could probably have been improved to an acceptable level. However, in view of the poor and deteriorating market environment, it was considered unlikely that an acceptable return in the future was obtainable. It is pertinent to mention here that prices had held reasonably constant over the period investigated and hence no inflation factor had to be built into the model. However, production and selling costs had increased over the same period and hence margins on sales had eroded. This meant that while the division could still get good margins on the major contracts, those obtainable from the smaller orders would be low. Since the physical number of major contracts available to the division was declining the pricing model could not retrieve the situation.

Estimates of future profits, using the model, were made and the expected net present value was calculated. This compared favourably with the other alternatives but the probability of achieving the required level of profitability was not very high.

7. *Expanding the product range to take the business into new market segments*

This alternative was partially discussed under the acquisition alternative. Since an acquisition would be the most logical vehicle for such expansion this alternative was considered to be redundant. Other product areas were outside the present manufacturing capabilities and hence significant capital investment would be required taking the business into markets in which the management had little relevant expertise.

8. *Running down the business and closing*

All that was necessary here was to calculate the costs of closure and the working capital that could be retrieved from the business. The beneficial effects of tax allowance on write-offs against reserves was taken into account and it was assumed that the working capital could be invested in a more favourable part of the company. This led to an expected net present value of future profits significantly above the acceptable level.

9. *Closing down manufacture and continuing as a design consultant*

No reliable information was available as to the likely demand for a design consultant in this industry and hence the alternative was not evaluated. However, this could be regarded as a later decision subsequent to the decision to close.

Although in many cases it was difficult to put precise values on the outcomes of choosing specific acts, it was fairly obvious that the best decision alternative, excluding closure, was to increase efficiency by improving the marketing performance. However, even in this case the probability of an acceptable return being earned was fairly low. Since the closure alternative would result in a financial return significantly above the acceptable level, it was undoubtedly the right decision to make on financial grounds.

Once a proper financial analysis was complete, non-financial considerations of the chosen act needed to be investigated. In this particular case, most of the production workers could be absorbed into other parts of the organisation. Some members of the staff would be made redundant but the total numbers were small. There was also no reason why the company should not pay severance pay to personnel made redundant, quite apart from the normal payments. This would certainly be true where there were substantial financial advantages in closing the business.

The development of the pricing and bidding model played an important role in this disinvestment decision in that it was used as an analytical tool and that its development raised many important questions, relating to market factors. However, the model was not eventually used in the bidding situation because of the closure of the business. Its real value was in removing part of the uncertainty inherent in the problem.

CHAPTER 8

Case Study 2—A Company Acquisition

INTRODUCTION

A large corporation may quite possibly average several acquisitions a year, but if the reader is not concerned with a large business, an acquisition case study may seem irrelevant. However the general approach used is applicable to most major investment decisions. The information sought will obviously vary according to the problem but the way it is used to evaluate alternative decisions is a common feature.

As in the last study, the inclusion of details relating to a specific acquisition study contravenes confidentiality requirements. Hence the study is an amalgam of several which were in fact made.

The problem arose in the first place because of explicit company objectives of expanding its interests in a particular direction. This direction was essentially to build on the strengths that already existed in a particular industry. A coarse informal sieve existed which sifted out many possible candidates and those that came through the basic criteria were then studied in depth.

These basic criteria were mainly concerned with size and growth in turnover and profitability, assessment of management ability, possible synergistic benefits and acceptability to the management of the group into which the acquired company would be incorporated. The last feature meant that many possible candidates were often first suggested by operating group management.

The present case arose through operating group management and therefore the criterion of acceptability was satisfied given that the company could be acquired for a price which compared favourably with its expected worth. From what was already known of the company the evidence suggested that it was run by competent management and it was thought that both management and the product mix would fit well with the existing business. There were clearly some areas of product overlap which would probably require rationalising but in general the products were of a complementary nature. Since these were sold to the same market segments it meant that the host company would be able to offer a more comprehensive range and probably be able to rationalise the marketing and selling functions of the two businesses.

Clearly there was sufficient information to suggest that such an acquisition would be in accord with long-term objectives and provide a reasonable return on the investment made. It was also thought that the company's shareholders and management would find the idea of merging with a large company very attractive since there were signs that their past growth rate could not be continued without seeking new sources of finance.

Another important feature of the situation was that the two businesses between them accounted for a large share of the United Kingdom market in one of the fastest growing lines. Hence a merger would decrease United Kingdom competition in this field by a significant amount. This in turn would permit stronger efforts to be made on the export front—with particular reference to the United States and Japanese markets. The European markets were already being handled by subsidiaries of each business located in different countries.

The past history of the two businesses was in general one of reasonably friendly competition although this had varied from a period when there was a serious price war to a later period when there was intercompany discussion on prices. However it was recognised that the current friendliness could quickly disappear if one business gained a strong technological advantage on the other. In fact the host company appeared to be in a stronger technological position—although its profit record was not quite as good as the other. This technological advantage was the recent development of a product which was thought to be a considerable improvement on anything else available. Since it offered some considerable advantages at a price only slightly higher than existing products the host company would be in a strong position to compete with the other company. However, the real motivation was to partially free the home market from competition in this area to allow stronger efforts to be directed towards export markets.

ISOLATION OF THE PROBLEM

The real problem, of course, was to decide whether to bid for the company and if so, what sort of price should be offered. This meant evaluating the worth of the company to the host business as well as evaluating its inherent worth to the market as a whole. There can, and often are, considerable differences in such evaluations of worth. As a simple analogy a threepenny piece is inherently worth three pennies to most people. If however a collector requires that particular coin to complete his collection he may very well pay much more. Indeed some rare coins are worth many thousand times their face value to certain collectors. In a similar way the worth of a company depends upon who is buying and yet it is necessary to calculate its inherent worth so that it can be appreciated just how big a premium is being paid.

It therefore follows that to answer the question of whether to bid and if so at what price, it was necessary to evaluate firstly the inherent worth of the company, and secondly the extra worth of it because of synergistic and rationalisation benefits and finally the premium that it may be worth paying to satisfy some strategic considerations. It is difficult to estimate the inherent value of a business, let alone the other values, but some effort must be made at establishing them. The discipline of attempting it will almost certainly provide a truer picture of the situation. Even if no estimate were eventually made of, say, the acceptable premium which it was worth paying, the exercise of trying to establish it will generally enable a far better understanding to be obtained of the business and the environment in which it operates.

A further set of problems also arise. These include forecasting the likely levels of turnover and profit over a given time period; evaluating the likely future market demand patterns; forecasting likely changes in the industry structure and so on. Since the main criterion is the level of future profits which the company will make, then the factors which may influence these levels, either adversely or favourably, need to be considered. In some cases forecasts will be required about these factors themselves, for example total market demand, and in other cases it may be possible to discern events now occurring which will have a future impact. For example if it were known that a technological breakthrough for a given process may render obsolete the present method then the stage reached in development at present needs to be looked at closely. A good example of this is in the printing industry where a breakthrough in gravure cylinder preparation could in the long term reverse the trend towards using offset lithography. The latter process has itself already partially displaced the letterpress process in some printing segments especially in the United States. The implications of such fundamental changes in production by the printer not only affects the manufacturers of presses but also the suppliers of materials and supplies. These effects go right through to the paper and other basic industries.

To just say that the problem is to evaluate the worth of the company and hence decide whether to bid for it or not is an over-simplification. In fact there must always be alternative strategies which the organisation can adopt to attempt to reach its objectives. The actual problem can only be defined precisely within the overall constraints imposed by the company's objectives. Those which are applicable are summarised as follows:

To become the leading manufacturer in the United Kingdom of a given set of products—in terms of market share.

To maintain the growth rate experienced in the past by this business, for the period five years ahead.

To maintain at least the current margins on sales and to increase pretax profits by at least the rate of growth in turnover.

To improve the return on capital employed to a specified level by the end of the five year period.

Within the five year period to become a major exporter especially to the U.S. and Japanese markets.

13

To maintain at least current levels of employment as far as is possible.

Clearly the acquisition of a suitable company or companies is one way to meet these strategic objectives. Other ways may include significant capital investment in plant, machinery or new premises and may involve opening production units overseas. Alternatively the objectives may be reached by undertaking a strong programme of research and development designed to result in significant product improvements. Equally, a strong programme of advertising promotions and building up sales outlets or dealers may reach the same objectives given that this is accompanied by investment in fixed assets so that production capacity is sufficient.

In practice the attainment of the objectives will usually be a combination of some or all of the above approaches. Hence what started as a straightforward question of whether to bid for company X or not in fact became a total evaluation of the strategies to pursue to attain the laid down corporate objectives. This point is of tremendous importance because the treatment of an acquisition prospect in a vacuum may easily result in an anomalous situation. History is dotted with many examples of companies being acquired only to find that, for example, its profits came mainly from an activity, possibly a subsidiary, which just failed to fit in with corporate objectives. Other cases are where companies are bought on a current rising trend of profits at the current price/earnings multiple, only to find that significant market changes were taking place even at that time and the result is that profits turn down two years later, and the acquired company becomes a liability. If management really know their business and realistic corporate objectives are laid down, then the evaluation of the worth of making an acquisition against various alternative strategies, can be attempted. If these conditions are absent then growth by acquisition may be dangerous in the long term. There are plenty of examples of companies which grew rapidly in the late fifties and early sixties by a programme of acquisitions and have been on a growth and profits plateau for the past five years. This is simply the outcome of adopting a strategy of buying short-term profits at the expense of building strong foundations for the longer-term prospects.

Probably the supreme example of a company setting corporate objectives and obtaining them in terms of growth, profitability and return to shareholders is the American company Harris-Intertype. This company has openly set its objectives and equally openly succeeded in maintaining them for at least the last fifteen years. These have been obtained by acquisition, product development, capital investment in expansion and last, but not least, a sustained marketing effort. Since the company is a technological leader in its two main fields—printing machinery and electronics—there is no reason to suppose that it will not continue to set realistic objectives and maintain them.

The various alternatives which faced senior management may briefly be summarised as follows:

1. Acquire company X.
2. Acquire an alternative company B.
3. Expand present production capacity at home.
4. Build production units overseas.
5. Institute a strong marketing programme.
6. Introduce the new product at a very competitive price and force their leading competitors to come to terms—that is either diversify into other activities or seek a merger on terms advantageous to the company.

The above six alternatives are what may be termed present or first order decisions. Since the problem has been set in the context of corporate objectives over a five year period, the six alternatives above are gross over-simplifications. For example if company X were acquired now, decisions will need to be made later as to whether to increase production capacity at home or build manufacturing units overseas. Alternatively such a purchase now may be followed by a further acquisition in say three years' time. All this is saying is that in the context of strategic considerations, decision making is sequential. Further, some of the above alternatives are mutually exclusive in the time sense while other orders are not. For example while it is possible to adopt alternative 6 now and alternative 1 later, it is not possible to adopt alternative 1 now and 6 later if company X were the only leading competitor.

There were other important decisions to be made if it were decided to acquire company X. The way in which the project should be financed would be of the utmost importance. If, for example, success depended upon a new equity issue and if the market were highly unfavourable at that time, then the decision to acquire the company may have to be deferred.

These are just a few examples of the way in which an acquisition problem can get very complex. As with most complex problems it is best to tackle the central issue first and to try to fit in the other requirements as progress is made. In this case the central issue was evaluating the worth of the company and this evaluation depended upon forecasting performance several years ahead.

To avoid becoming immersed in too complex a problem it was sub-divided into two distinct information gathering and analytical approaches, which proceeded simultaneously. The gathering exercise related to an assessment of the operating environment and technological developments. The analytical approach was an examination of the company's historical operating characteristics and used this to build a model representing their business. The intention was to carry out these exercises more or less independently and then fit the operating model into the environmental picture. Although these studies continued at the same time, each is discussed separately. One person was intimately involved in both operations over the whole period and was therefore able to co-ordinate the activities. In particular, market information was obtained from time to time which meant that short cuts could be taken in the construction of the model. The analytical approach prompted questions which were explored in the market.

It could be argued that the best approach in a case such as this is not necessarily the simultaneous execution of the information gathering process and analysis of historical information. In the absence of time constraints this argument is valid and indeed the previous case history proceeded more logically although there was considerable overlap. However, there was a fairly rigid deadline and hence every effort was made to minimise the time

taken while avoiding as far as possible doing abortive exercises·
The information gathering part of the exercise is described in
the next section, although reference is made from time to time
to the analytical exercise since this prompted some of the information work.

THE ENVIRONMENTAL STUDY

The object of this study was to gather information relating to the
environment within which company X operated and also
adjacent fields where technological developments could affect
the markets of the company.

These objectives and the way in which they were handled are
briefly discussed one by one to show the sources and nature of
information required and how quantitative analyses were
carried out.

1. *Size of the United Kingdom market and export markets*

Broad industry statistics were available for the United
Kingdom market in the Monthly Digest of Statistics and a further breakdown for a limited past period in one of the Business
Monitor Series. The last Census of Production published—that
is the 1963 Census, gave detailed information for that year as did
the 1958 report. Although this was some help it was too far out
of date to be more than just a guide. Nevertheless a broad
industry picture was obtained from these sources, the Annual
Abstract of Statistics, and relevant Business Monitor series.

The next step was to find out whether there were any appropriate trade associations. Several were located and one of these
had recently conducted a fairly comprehensive survey of one
product area. A summarised form of these results was bought
from the association concerned and information was obtained
for that product and also some information relating to others.
Although the other trade associations were unable to give much
help they did provide some contacts which were added to those
which had been obtained from the divisional management.

While these enquiries were being conducted, the names of
useful looking periodicals had been extracted from *Flannans*

Pocket Media Guide and copies of each had been ordered. These provided a wealth of information, including the fact that one of the areas of interest had been surveyed by one of the Economic Development Committees. A telephone call to this department resulted in a great deal of information being offered, some of which was highly relevant.

Having exhausted these sources a day was spent at the Patent Office Library and further sources were located from back numbers of trade periodicals. These were systematically scanned and provided considerable information.

To get sales statistics for overseas companies, visits were paid to the relevant Embassies and Chambers of Commerce. Detailed statistics were obtained for America and Japan, in the case of the latter, a complete report on the appropriate markets was located, and broad industry statistics were obtained for most of the other applicable countries.

The next step was to explore the list of personal contacts which had been built up. These contacts were amongst competitors, companies that served the same markets but do not compete, major customers, universities and colleges of technology. Even trade union headquarters were approached.

The desk research exercise allowed a fairly good picture of much of the market to be built up and extensive information was also obtained relating to the other objectives. However, there was one important product area for which demand statistics had not been obtained. This problem was approached in two ways. The first was by analogy with the American market for which detailed statistics were available. The second was to extract the companies listed in the directory *Kompass* as producing the product in question. Copies of their accounts were obtained where possible and from these an estimate of production was made. Since some of these companies were in fact customers of other parts of the group it was possible to get detailed production information in some cases. It was felt that the estimates made, which were within 10 per cent of the estimate made by analogy to the American market, were sufficiently accurate to be useful.

One point worth making is that it may be hazardous to rely exclusively on an analogy to the American market. In this particular case the product in question was used by another industry and an econometric relationship was found between changes in this industry and changes in demand for the product in the American data. This relationship was applied to the United Kingdom statistics and it proved to be a good estimator.

2. *Size and growth of each product segment broken down by user and geographical segment*

The research described provided sufficient data to estimate total home and export demand for each of the company's main products. It also permitted the historic growth rates to be measured, but in most cases it had not been possible to get a breakdown by user segment or geographically.

Some of the products had been covered comprehensively by the market reports which had been obtained, but there were three important cases for which information was not available. It was established from the trade directory *Kompass* that the companies which manufactured these products tended to supply all of them and it was not difficult to determine the 20 major manufacturers which together with company X probably accounted for 80 per cent of home production. However, there was little prospect of getting information from many of these since this sort of market information is usually only obtainable by carrying out an expensive survey. Certainly it was not considered important enough for the decisions that had to be made to spend much time or money on the problem and therefore carrying out a survey was not considered. However a quick perusal of trade literature led to the conclusion that there were two principal industrial users and considerable information was available on these industrial segments. Hopefully, it was assumed that the growth rate of the products in question was the same as the industrial segments and that the value of sales to each was proportional to the relative sizes of these two industries.

3. *Isolating the factors which influence demand*

Again considerable information had already been obtained

from published information. This was not quite sufficient and hence the views of major users, where known, were sought by a short programme of personal interviews. This also produced further information on the user segments, but there was insufficient time to explore this deeply.

From the information gathered each product was specified in terms of the way in which it was used, the principal technical or commercial features which were sought—that is price, quality, reliability, fast delivery and others—and how the products of competitors compared with each other.

4. *Evaluating changing patterns of demand*

In most cases sufficient information had been obtained from the sources already mentioned on this topic. However, the only way of discerning changes in some areas would have been to do a full market survey and this was not possible in the time available. The interview programme provided a considerable number of detailed views on the way things were likely to develop and although some were contradictory, these proved to be very useful in assessing the long-term trends.

5. *Forecasting demand for five years ahead*

Some long term forecasts had been obtained during the information gathering process. Independent forecasts were made for the individual product segments on a trend basis—taking into account the likelihood of a trade recession in the period 1971/2. These were backed up by forecasts for groups of similar products based on relationships, with demand for the industrial equipment for which these products were used. Using official forecasts for these industries in some cases and in others relating them to Gross National Product, forecasts were made for these aggregates. Statistical standard errors were calculated for each year on the basis of the equations used, and these permitted ranges to be given as well as the expected demand. In addition these forecasts were examined by one of the company's experts on that industry and the confidence limits were widened or narrowed according to his views.

6. *Estimation of the market shares of company X and the leading competitors*

This was simple in the case of company X for detailed sales statistics were available. For the competitors it was a matter of rough estimation using their accounts or any other information which had been obtained.

7. *Examination of the main competitors' operating characteristics*

This examination consisted of calculating historic growth rates in turnover and profits, margins and return on net capital employed. In addition ratios were calculated for the most important characteristics—that is Sales to Net Fixed Assets, Sales to Stocks, Sales to Debtors, Debtors to Creditors, Current Assets to Current Liabilities—and the industry averages were computed. A publication called *Business Ratios* was very helpful.

8. *Examination of methods of production and technological developments amongst the competitors*

Again considerable information was obtained from trade publications, going back two years. This of course is very time consuming but can be very rewarding since companies often announce the installation of new plant and machinery and certainly publicise their technological developments. In addition magazines like *New Scientist, Technology* and special reports which appear in papers like the *Financial Times* yield a tremendous amount of information. The latter in particular is often used by companies to proclaim their technological endeavours.

9. *Determination of whether it is an easy-access field*

The ease with which companies can enter markets depends to a considerable extent on the extent of patent protection and the cost of setting up production—that is the capital investment required for premises, plant and machinery. In the case in question it was a field of moderately high technology with limited access.

The numbers of new entrants were approximately determined by looking at successive years of trade directories.

10. *Determination of special industry requirements*

There were several special features of the industry in question —one in particular related to methods of distribution. Since the trade press discussed the industry problems in some detail it was felt that sufficient information had been obtained. Besides which, the company's own activities in some of the relevant industries were fairly extensive.

11. *Future manpower requirements*

From the companies' accounts, which had been collected, it was easy to relate changes in total requirements to growth in output. Knowing from an internal evaluation that value added represented a large proportion of output it was easy to guess the proportion of direct labour. In fact time was wasted here because much better data was obtained from the Ministry of Labour.

Very rough predictions were made of future equirements for the industry and it was thought that sufficient manpower resources would be available over the period considered except for specialist functions such as computer and design staff. It was considered that this constituted a cost which should be taken into account since the industry was computer orientated and required considerable design skills. Wage rates for these two categories were likely to rise at a rate considerably above the average and further some provision should be made for training staff to fulfil these functions.

Detailed sales forecasts were produced and from the competitor information, forecasts were also made for profits. From the trends in capital employed, industry cash flows were calculated and these appeared to be more than adequate to support the expected rate of growth.

In addition, various averages and ranges of the key industrial ratios were calculated.

THE ANALYSIS OF COMPANY X'S INTERNAL OPERATING
CHARACTERISTICS

Since the study included detailed demand forecasts and estimates
of future levels of profit expected to be earned by the industry,
it was necessary to compare company X's performance with the
overall industry performance, and to determine future requirements for cash resources given that specified levels of growth
were to be achieved.

Hence the problem was essentially to estimate for a period of
five years ahead likely levels of sales, profits and financial inputs
required. The problem was approached by doing two separate
exercises and reconciling the results.

Detailed sales forecasts product by product on a trend or
econometric basis were made using six years historical
information. These were made having regard to market
shares and relative competitive strengths and were aggregated
into one composite forecast for each year over the five year
period.

The construction of a model representing the internal operating characteristics which would be used for forecasting sales,
profits and financial inputs.

For both exercises information was sought on the company's
technological position and the likelihood of it maintaining its
competitive position. In addition further work was required to
attempt to assess possible synergistic benefits which would be
obtained by merging and the extent to which the two sets of
management could be integrated successfully. A probability
distribution of the worth of the company was required. It is not
enough to estimate the company's expected worth alone since
this does not permit a realistic estimate of the risks involved to
be made.

Product sales forecasts

Since company X had itself acquired subsidiaries over the past
five years only one or two years data was available for some

products. These tended to constitute a relatively small proportion of the total and hence forecasts were made on the basis of
the appropriate industry rate of growth—that is assuming a
constant share of United Kingdom production.

The other products were classified into order of importance
as measured by the proportion of total sales. Those which had
some outstanding features such as considerable technical advantage, or being in a very high growth market were grouped
with the main products to account altogether for 75 per cent of
the company's sales.

The products which accounted for the remaining 25 per cent
tended to exhibit static or declining growth and in most cases
this reflected the overall market. Forecasts for each of these were
based on trend fitting methods. Where a cyclic effect existed, a
simple sinusoidal wave form was added to the trend to approximately simulate the cycle. In each case, constant market share
was assumed. Where a decline in sales was occurring, an acceptable threshold level was assumed. At the point in time when
sales fell below this level and if the decline reflected the overall
industry, the product was assumed to be withdrawn from production.

Using a computer time sharing terminal these forecasts were
completed very quickly since sufficient ground work had been
completed in advance so that the right program packages
could be immediately selected.

The next products considered were those which had some outstanding features. In one particular case the product accounted
for a significant proportion of total sales and had been growing
at an average compound rate of 25 per cent per annum. Since
it was known that company X's sales of this product together
with the host company's equivalent sales, which were growing
at 30 per cent per annum, accounted for over 50 per cent of the
United Kingdom market which itself was growing at 15 per
cent per annum, it was clear that these growth rates could not
be maintained indefinitely.

In *Figure 19* the total market forecasts for this product are
shown for five years ahead based on an index of 100 units at
present. The overall growth rate is at 15 per cent per annum
excluding the third period which corresponds with a cyclic

downturn. Clearly if sales of the two companies combined continued even at the lower rate of the two, that is 25 per cent per annum, the combined market share would reach over 90 per cent by the end of the sixth year, and this was thought to be highly unlikely. Hence a restriction of a 75 per cent market share was assumed and growth of the combined business was assumed at 25 per cent until this restriction occurred and then further growth continued at 15 per cent per annum.

Another product was a recent development of one of company X's recent acquisitions and hence very limited data was available. Divisional management expressed the opinion that a significant market share could be obtained with it over a five year period—that is a 20 per cent market share. The analyst's opinion was that this was over-optimistic and forecasts were made on the alternative assumptions that sales of the product reached 5, 10, 15 and 20 per cent over this period. Logistic type curves were used to specify these alternatives in mathematical form.

In one other product area, an important one to the company,

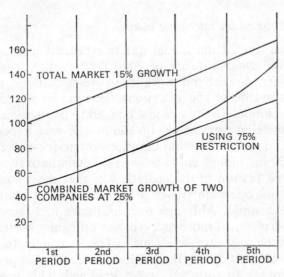

Figure 19

SALES GROWTH RESTRICTED BY TOTAL MARKET GROWTH

it was found that sales were closely related to the installation rate of digital computers on a one year lagged basis. A simple econometric relationship was found which provided very precise estimates one year ahead. For the remaining periods, estimates had to be made of changes in new orders for computers so that the demand for the product could be assessed.

By employing suitable techniques as described in each case and using the information gathered during the market environment appraisal, forecasts were made for each product. Some of these were altered as further information became available, and some measure of the forecasting precision was made. The latter ranged from the mathematical calculation of standard errors, to estimates of upper and lower limits based on expert market judgements. The separate forecasts were aggregated into one composite forecast and some approximations to the standard errors of the estimates were made. These permitted the formulation of probability distributions for the total sales forecasts to be made for each year. The shapes of the distributions were assumed to be symmetrical.

Construction of an operating model

The purpose of the model was to represent mathematically past performance in terms of sales, profits, current assets, net fixed assets, stocks and work-in-progress, debtors, creditors, dividend payments and retentions. This model would then be put on a computerised basis and be used to predict sales, profits and financial requirements. In addition it was hoped that it could be constructed so that the affects on performance of altering the capital inputs, could be assessed quantitatively.

The first feature in the analysis was that the company had financed its operations over a ten year period mainly from retained earnings. Although one debenture had recently been issued this was used more or less to pay off bank overdraft which at that time was excessively high. The second feature of the business was that during the first half of the ten year period very strong growth in turnover was maintained. This was accompanied by an even faster growth in net fixed assets and much slower growth in current assets. It was believed that the high growth rate during this period was due to a conscious policy on the part of the management to increase turnover by expanding production capacity mainly on the home market. In the second five year period, even faster growth in turnover was achieved and this was accompanied by a relatively slow increase in net fixed assets but a much faster rate of growth in current assets. It was believed that the company's growth over this period was the result of deliberate policy decisions to expand overseas and the main vehicle for expansion was by acquisition, although some acquisitions on the home market had been made.

Clearly there were two distinct 'histories' in the ten year figures and hence any model based on the whole of this data would predict average affects of the two policies. Since it was not known whether any major policy change would occur, this in itself was reasonable. However, in addition to the 'average effect' model, less sophisticated models were based on two alternative assumptions, one, that the present policy continued and two, that the previous policy of expansion by increasing production capacity was again adopted. These two assumptions would then yield notional upper and lower estimates in addition to those provided by the model on a statistical basis.

From the historical data it could be seen that growth in total assets—that is current assets $+$ net fixed assets was related very closely to accumulated retained earnings lagged by one year, that is total assets at the end of year t, depended upon the levels of retentions in each period to the end of year $t - 1$. This is to be expected in an auto-financing situation and hence the exceptionally close empirical relationship was supported on logical grounds.

It was found that the level of sales at the end of year t depended upon total assets at that time and the position in the economic cycle. The relationship between these two variables was approximately linear with a wave form superimposed on it to represent the cyclic affect.

A further linear relationship was found between end of year sales and trading profits, that is profits before depreciation, interest charges, tax and dividend payments. Net fixed assets were derived from sales, using a linear equation, and depreciation was derived from net fixed assets using a constant ratio.

Interest charges were negligible and tax was calculated at the standard corporation tax level. There was an approximate two year lag between tax being due and it being paid and this was taken into account in the model.

Dividend payments were calculated on the basis that the recent policy of growth in dividend payments would be continued. A restriction was built into the model to prevent divident payments exceeding a certain proportion of after-tax profits. Whenever this restriction was used, the payments would equal those made in the previous year. In other words the pay-out ratio may exceed this specified proportion but there would be no absolute increase over the previous period.

Hence, after-tax profits, dividend payments and thus retained earnings could be calculated.

Since the accumulated retained earnings were known at the end of the past year, this data could be used in the model to predict total assets at the end of the current year. This could then be used to predict sales at the same point in time and this in turn would be used to derive trading profits and after-tax profits. From the dividend assumptions, retained earnings could be calculated and hence accumulated retentions at that time. Having calculated the accumulated retentions at the end of this year, that estimate was then used to predict the following year's assets. The process was continued until forecasts for each year in the five year period had been made.

This model was the first approach and was followed by further developments, along the same lines, which took into account creditors, debtors, stocks and work-in-progress and bank over-draft. This was eventually used to evaluate future performance. The flow diagram for the simple model is shown in *Figure 20*.

The way the model was used was as a predictor of future levels of sales and profits and to estimate the effects of varying financial inputs and changes in dividend policy or other policy changes. To do this a computer program was prepared which included the equations formulated. A complete set of sales and profit forecasts was obtained. The sales forecasts were reasonably close to those made on the aggregate basis described earlier.

The next step was to consider changes in financial inputs and see what affect these had on sales and profits. This of course had to be considered against the environmental background. Subsequently the affects of changes in dividend policy were also evaluated.

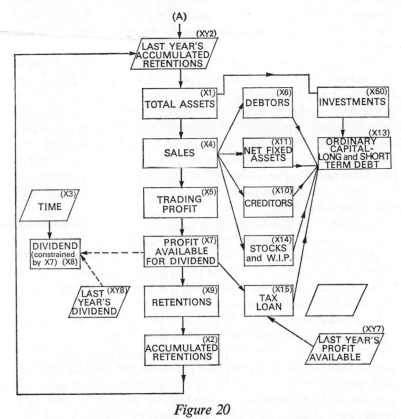

Figure 20

PREDICTING FUTURE LEVELS OF SALES AND PROFITS

The last step was to take into account the two alternative growth strategies discussed earlier. These were dealt with in a simple way, by constructing one model based on the first five years' data and the other on the second five year's.

By the time the exercise was complete a very good idea of the different possibilities had been obtained. In other words a number of possible different futures had been enumerated but of course there was no way of knowing for sure which one in particular would occur. In addition, the forecasts obtained in the worst possible case were considerably lower than in the most favourable case. However, most of the results centred fairly closely around a set of mean values and, in the case of the sales estimates, these were reasonably close to the predictions made on the aggregate basis.

The distribution of the different forecasts was plotted out in the form of a histogram and this actual plot was used to estimate the probability that profits would lie within a given range. Each profit level was accompanied by depreciation levels and levels of net capital employed and hence cash flows were calculated for each year. These were discounted at a rate which reflected the cost of capital, assuming a perpetuity from the end of the five year period. The probability obtained from the histogram was applied to the net present value so calculated until all cases had been dealt with.

From these calculations the expected worth of the company was calculated, by multiplying each net present value by its probability of occurring. The data was then used to estimate the probability that the net present value of the company would lie between different levels. This enabled the calculation of a level which would be exceeded with a probability of 80 per cent.

In the absence of other information the value of the company to the host company would lie between the 80 per cent level and the expected value. Clearly the closer the sum paid is to the expected value of the company, the greater is the risk that the host company takes. In this particular study there were considerable benefits to be derived from rationalising production and sales functions including the distribution network. Estimates of these savings had also to be made and taken into account.

Ultimately a value is attached to the potential acquisition which corresponds with a low risk to the host company, and would be considered as very advantageous. The highest price worth paying would probably be its expected value. However, if there existed strong strategic considerations there may very well be good arguments for paying a high premium. At least the cost of this premium can be evaluated if the sort of study discussed has been properly performed.

THE DECISION MAKING PROCESS

Firstly, the acquisition of company X had to be considered against the background of corporate objectives as mentioned. Following this it was necessary to compare the acquisition with various other alternatives which could also result in these objectives being achieved, if adopted.

The first objective, to become the leading manufacturer in the United Kingdom in this field, would be achieved if the acquisition went through, for most of the specified products. For other products there would still need to be further market penetration—but this would be achievable relatively easily.

The objective of maintaining the record of growth in turnover would have a high probability of being achieved. This following directly from the market demand study and the sales forecasts made.

The next objective referred to maintenance of margins on sales. From the profit forecasts made it was thought that margins generally might experience a slight decline on average over the five year period. Against this, however, there were various benefits to be derived from merging the two businesses and rationalising production and distribution systems. From the calculations made it was thought that margins for the combined business could even be improved. Hence this objective appeared to be satisfied.

The objective, to improve the return on net capital employed over the five year period, should be maintained since both profits and net capital employed had been derived from the model and using these estimates together with the additional profits arising from rationalisation, it was possible to predict the return on net capital employed for each year.

The five year plan to become a major exporter was more difficult to evaluate. The exports of company X represented a relatively small proportion of their total sales, although the rate of increase was very rapid because of the recent acquisition programme which had been pursued. The real merit of the acquisition in this respect was that it removed a substantial slice of the competition in certain product areas on the home market and hence permitted an all out export drive. It was thought that this objective could be achieved with a fairly high probability.

The last objective specified, to maintain present levels of employment, was considered readily attainable. However, it was recognised that initial rationalisation could result in an initial drop in numbers employed. It was thought that this fall could be met mainly by retirements and natural wastage.

The principal objectives would be achieved by acquiring company X. However, these objectives were also achievable by adopting other strategies. These other strategies constituted the other decision alternatives before senior management, although some of them became redundant as a result of the studies carried out. For example, from the information gathered there did not appear to be a more suitable acquisition candidate. However there was just not time to evaluate the performance of each possible candidate in the same depth, but certainly no other United Kingdom competitor either fitted so well in terms of its product range or management or had such a successful performance record.

The real alternatives before senior management were therefore reduced to:

1. Buy company X and expand production capacity at home and possibly abroad.

2. Do not buy company X but expand capacity by extra amount necessary to meet the specified objectives.

3. Introduce the new product at a very competitive price and attempt to force company X to seek a merger on more advantageous terms.

The first alternative has already been explored in depth and the probability of the integration of the two businesses ending in failure had been calculated. Failure here means in terms of the desired objectives. However, there still remained the future decision to open a production unit overseas. Since the main overseas markets had been studied and a comparison had been made between competitive products, the probability of the venture being successful could be estimated. All that was now required was an estimate of the likely capital investment involved in this future decision.

For the second alternative the cost of expanding capacity had to be estimated. In addition this alternative meant that in the not too distant future there would be a head on clash with company X who were the most likely to suffer from attempts at increasing market shares. This clash might lead to a price war, which had occurred in the past, and this would in turn result at least for a period, in diminished profits and possibly a slowing down in the sales growth rate in value terms.

The third alternative was not considered acceptable on grounds of 'personal preference', but since it was necessary to consider the cost of keeping to a high ethical code, the alternative was evaluated. The evaluation was essentially to assess the likely affect of this policy on company X's margins and sales over a two year period and extrapolate this affect over a longer period—that is diminishing the profits predicted by the model

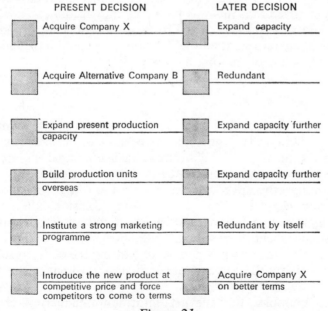

Figure 21

THE DECISION ALTERNATIVES IN THE AQUISITION PROBLEM

by the proportion calculated. The net present value of the company under these circumstances was then calculated. The cost of the company was taken as the sum of this net present value and the loss of profits which would be incurred over the first two years.

Not much effort was put into evaluating the third alternative although it was thought that if the strategy were successful it could have resulted in a substantial saving. Against this however there was the chance that such an action could precipitate industrial rationalisation amongst competitors to form a very strong group which would increase competition further. The alternative was therefore ruled out mainly on these grounds so the problem became the choice of buying company X and expanding capacity later, or attempting to achieve objectives by a programme of internal expansion and/or improvement in operating efficiency.

Figure 21 demonstrates the alternatives available. Note that the cost of the investigation was so small compared with the sums involved that this was not taken into account at any stage in the decision process. If the cost were a significant proportion of the likely returns then the decision tree would have included the alternative of making no study.

CONCLUDING REMARKS

The main purpose in including this acquisition case study has been to demonstrate the approach to a major business problem. Since the principles of discounted cash flow analysis are very widely known and documented these were omitted.

Although the approach was within the format expanded in previous chapters—that is, problem, decision alternatives, information, predictions and choice of acts—it is obvious that various short cuts were taken. These short cuts were all in accordance with the general principle of 'cutting the cloth to suit the purse'—that is the compromise of analytical rigour to stay within the bounds set by reality.

For example, the market information-gathering exercise proceeded simultaneously with the historical analysis. Perhaps ideally the historical analysis should always be attempted first so that more precise information requirements may be stated. In practice it is very much a question of the time available. In this particular case by using a strong co-ordinating link, very little efficiency was lost and considerable time was saved.

Another short cut was the way in which some decision alternatives were made redundant or dismissed on the basis of relatively little investigation. Again under ideal conditions this would not be done; nor indeed would the cost of the investigation be left out of the calculations. However, it is always necessary to balance expediency with rigour. In doing this it is often the analyst's job to use his expert judgement to decide just how much expediency is acceptable and how much rigour he can omit. There are few guide lines which can be laid down here although if the analyst really believes that a particular piece of work should be done then he must make his own opinion heard. This may be difficult when powerful voices are clamouring for analytical results but the analyst is in a unique position and ultimately the decision choice may rest heavily upon his anlaysis and interpretation.

Apart from the shortcomings of the work done, the analysis only provided a rational way of making the choice of whether to bid for company X or not. It did of course provide an estimate of the maximum price which should be paid and also what sort of price would constitue a 'good buy'. It could not, however, nor is there much likelihood that the analytical approach ever will, provide a framework for negotiating. This is really a strictly qualitative function although of course the various investigations provided the negotiator with considerable information. If the negotiator knows practically as much about the potential acquisition as that company's own management then he is not likely to be out-negotiated. Once the opposition learn that he is well briefed they will tread carefully.

Have the following factors and elements been assessed and the results set down in writing? 'The company' is the company under examination for possible acquisition.

1. The products sold by the company.

2. The services provided by it.

3. The market segments in which the company operates.

4. The factors influencing demand.

5. Any changing patterns of demand.

6. The effect of the economic trade cycle.

7. Any exceptional non-recurring demand factors.

8. Types of customers served.

9. The main purchasing influence.

10. Sales to overseas markets.
    (*a*) present importance
    (*b*) probable future importance
    (*c*) profitability

11. Methods of distribution, e.g.,
    (*a*) at home
    (*b*) overseas
        e.g., (*i*) own sales force
            (*ii*) through wholesalers
            (*iii*) through factors
            (*iv*) through agents
            (*v*) manufactured under licence

12. The influence of any outside party other than customers on sales or production.

13. Any pending rationalisation of the industry.

14. Principal competitors in each product or service field.
   (*a*) comparative performance
   (*b*) their reputation in the industry
   (*c*) their reputation with customers

15. The company's operating characteristics compared with the overall industry.

16. The rate of technological innovation compared with other competitive companies.

17. R. & D. projects in the pipe-line (listed).

18. The rate at which new products have been marketed.

19. Design strengths (listed).

20. Product characteristics, e.g., reliability (listed).

21. The compatibility of the company's expertise with that of the host company.

22. Management strengths.

23. The sales of each product in each segment.

24. The extent of market penetration for each product.

25. The share of the market for each product.

26. The growth rate for each product.

27. Legal restraints and patents.

28. Pricing and discount policies.

29. Location of proposed acquisition.

30. Size of proposed acquisition.

31. Any surplus capacity.

32. Financial position.

33. How financed.

34. Forecasts for:
   (*a*) sales
   (*b*) profits
   (*c*) capital requirements

35. Benefit to be derived from integration.

36. The inherent worth of the company.

37. Its worth to the host company.

38. Maximum price the host is prepared to pay.

39. Has a negotiating strategy been worked out and outlined in writing?

40. Has a strategy been worked out and outlined in writing for incorporating and changing the company's management team?

CHAPTER 9

The Interaction of the Problem, Information and Prediction in Decision Making

THE UNIFIED APPROACH TO MARKETING

Marketing problems are a sub-class of the total set of all business problems. In a marketing-oriented company the realisation of the importance of marketing results in most problems being classified, at least partially, as marketing because some market information is usually required. However, the boundaries between so-called marketing problems and so-called financial or production problems are very ill-defined. This means that dealing with business problems on a functional basis is often unsatisfactory. For example the extreme cases of production-oriented companies of the late forties and fifties eventually managed to reach a philosophy where their prime purpose was to manufacture a product and only then consider whether or not there existed a real market for it. Now tremendous trouble may be taken to ensure that there is a need, or a need can be generated, for a product, before manufacture is started.

The position will probably one day be reached when companies in their enthusiasm will 'sell' products which possibly cannot be produced.

An inflexible division of an organisation functionally may lead to too narrow an outlook which then almost inevitably leads to inadequate use of the information available. It may therefore be better to resist the temptation to label problems as 'marketing' or 'production'. Instead, the simple label of business problems requiring marketing or production information is less misleading.

This is not to suggest that an organisation should not be divided up functionally for obviously the salesman has to sell and the buyer has to buy, but the division should reflect administrative responsibility, the responsibility for carrying out or implementing the decisions made, and the responsibility for the day-to-day decisions which are not serious enough to warrant much management attention or time. In addition, and very important, the functional separation should reflect information sources—that is the salesman in addition to selling must feed back market information; the personnel officer must feed back information on labour relations, wage rates and the labour market.

If there exists a strong central management service function armed with the necessary management skills and operating within a sound information system then it may be possible to bring to bear these skills along with those of the operating group personnel on the major problems which face the latter. This means that for major decisions, the central management service function becomes involved in an advisory, consultant, co-ordinating or monitoring role, or even possibly takes over the whole problem in some cases.

There are several advantages to this 'ideal' system. Possibly the most important is the cross-fertilisation affect which is brought about by bringing operating personnel into close contact with a variety of specialist management skills and with personnel from other parts of the business. Another considerable advantage is that it permits the formulation of an independent view by central management. This is essential in a situation where the operating divisions are financed from the centre and therefore have to provide strong cases to obtain funds. If there is strong competition for limited resources then relying solely on the picture painted by operating management may be hazardous. In the absence of a monitoring function, it is likely that often the division with the most articulate manager will get a disproportionate part of the total resources available. Naturally this could be against the interests of the total organisation.

Again in a system where divisional management does not have access to specialist skills, decisions may be taken in an unsophisticated way. It is likely that even if management has access to the necessary skills, they may not realise what is required because of their own lack of knowledge, and, hence do not call upon the available resources. This would hardly happen where major problems are considered independently by the central service department.

For such a system to work it is of course essential that not only is a comprehensive information system set up but also that full co-operation from operating management is obtained. Clearly there are many ways in which the systems can go wrong and only by very careful evaluation and implementation can the worst ones be avoided.

Probably the most significant factor which may cause failure is mistrust by the operating group personnel of the often unknown people in the central function. The amount of mistrust present is likely to be inversely proportional to the performance of the business. If the business is doing well they will bare their souls knowing that only virgin snow is discernible. If performance is bad, 'outsiders' will often be regarded as spies.

Another important factor may be the unwillingness of the central personnel to take the trouble to get a good understanding of the individual businesses and the environment in which they operate. Lack of fairly detailed knowledge of a specific business may result in a lack of understanding of the problems facing the division and hence lack of sympathy. Further, such a deficiency certainly does not equip a person, no matter what specialist skills he possesses, to help to any real extent. Operating group personnel are likely to think that their fears are justified, and would probably be right.

The importance of a good information system with two-way flow cannot be over-emphasised. In the absence of such a system, no real attempt can be made to run an organisation as suggested. The same criticism applies to the absence of proper financial and commercial control systems. Amongst various other factors geographical distance may be one consideration, although using computer information systems this should be readily overcome.

Another criticism, and it is very difficult to assess its importance, is the dilution of divisional managements' responsibility. If it could be accepted that the aim was to provide better facilities for their decision making and if their performance were geared to incentives and disincentives then some of these human relations problems may be minimised.

The clear message of this section is that it may be intrinsically wrong to classify business problems into functional categories. Clearly if the sort of organisation structure discussed is in operation, then labelling ceases to be important. However, this sort of structure invites disaster from any one of the possible adverse factors mentioned. By the same token, its adoption may result in vastly improved decision making. To obtain this it must be necessary to tread very warily indeed.

THE TEST OF GOOD DECISION MAKING

The mechanics of systematic decision making have been considered without discussing the deeper question of what constitutes a good decision. If it is accepted that the decision maker should systematically evaluate alternative courses of action, constrained by pre-determined criteria and availability of information then the role of logical analysis in this approach needs to be assessed.

It is not sufficient for the decision maker to just be consistent and systematic because if he fails to apply logical analysis he may systematically make the same mistakes and be consistently wrong. Even if he applies all three of these principles— systematic, consistent, logical analysis—he may only succeed in selecting the best alternative from an inferior sub-set of alternatives—simply because he failed to enumerate all the alternatives.

Since it is unlikely that all alternatives can ever be specified in any given case it follows that sometimes the 'best' solution will not be included. Equally, because it is unlikely that all possible events can be specified, then there will be cases where an important event is not taken into account. This 'sin of omission' as it was called in an earlier chapter probably applies to each stage in the decision making process and is difficult to obviate.

Because of the omission possibility, it follows that it is not possible to devise a decision-making system which will permit the 'best' alternative to be selected, even if perfect future knowledge were available. This is nothing to do with the probabilistic nature of decision making because even if 'certain knowledge' of future events were available it would not help to select the best alternative if this had been excluded from the set under consideration. Only the best of that sub-set would be chosen.

It may be argued that this state of affairs makes formal decision analysis redundant. The argument would be false, however, since the aim of the formal approach is not to select the best alternative in the absolute sense. It is rather intended to improve decision making and to do this systematically by using all available information in a logical manner. In addition, the formal approach, besides increasing understanding of the situation, provides a good learning system. If the decision maker in retrospect evaluates the decision process it is likely that he can beneficially adjust his thinking for the next case.

Having more or less written off the idea of obtaining the best decision, except in a very limited sense, the concept of a good decision requires further consideration. Some would argue that the 'proof of the pudding is in the eating' and hence a decision can only be judged as good or bad depending upon the favourability or otherwise of the result. This implies that a decision maker should be judged by his record of decision making.

In a sense it is true that ends often justify means, but in the context of rational decision making, of improving performance and understanding, the argument is false in the long run.

The decision maker who uses his judgement in a given situation may reasonably be accused of acting intuitively if he is unable to furnish reasons for his selection of a particular course of action. This is not necessarily saying that he was wrong, for he may just find it difficult to put into words the complex reasoning which perhaps preceded his choice. However, if sufficient time were available to gather applicable information or to tackle the problem more systematically then he may be criticised for failing to do so.

This criticism is essentially concerned with the actual process of decision making and even if the outcome in a particular case were highly favourable, this should not lessen the criticism. The fact is that adopting a formal approach to decision making not only lessens the chance of unfavourable outcomes, but in addition permits others to judge for themselves the reasonableness of the decision. After all, if all the evidence pointed to a particular event occurring, which would result in a highly favourable outcome if a specific decision alternative were selected, then it should be selected. Even in retrospect, when it is known that a low probability event occurred resulting in an unfavourable outcome, the decision which was made could not be considered bad. If the decision maker had used all the available information and estimated the probabilities reasonably then he was *right* to make that decision, even though the outcome turned out to be unfavourable.

This is an important idea because it is differentiating between the decision-making process and the outcome of that process.

To emphasise this concept, *Figure 22* demonstrates the alternatives that can happen. In reality there may be an infinite range of possibilities between good and bad. From the diagram

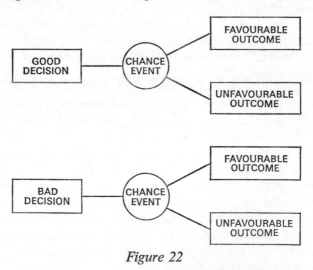

Figure 22

THE DIFFERENCE BETWEEN BAD DECISIONS
AND FAVOURABLE OUTCOMES

it can be seen that not only can a good decision have an unfavourable outcome, but a bad decision can have a favourable outcome.

If the decision maker were to analyse the problem and make the decision on logical and well thought out grounds, then the fact that the outcome was unfavourable does not mean that he made a bad decision. Since decision making is probabilistic it follows that there will always be some chance that the outcome is unfavourable. This in turn implies that any judgement of a decision maker should be based on evaluating the process he uses, rather than on the results of the decision.

If this differentiation between the decision and the outcome is thought to be pedantic and that the only practical way of evaluating decision making is on the results, the implications of this thinking should be considered. First, if a manager, who is basically deficient of the analytical qualities required, has a couple of strokes of luck he may move well beyond his level of competence. This may have the most seriously adverse consequences since he then influences more serious situations and further, if he is inadequate, will probably gather other inadequate people around him.

The converse of this situation also holds.

The manager with very good qualities may just as easily suffer some unfavourable outcomes and it may possibly set him back for some considerable period. Even more important is the fact that because it is difficult to judge how good a decision maker is, if decisions are not made in a formal manner, very often judgements will be made on totally different criteria which might be quite irrelevant to his skills as a decision maker.

Suppose however that a decision maker consistently made good decisions even though the decision process was not known. Should the empirical evidence be used to assess his abilities? The answer is probably that it should and this is in obvious disagreement with the above argument of judging on the basis of the decision-making process. To reconcile the apparent discrepancy further exploration is needed. Clearly where a new organisation is set up, the criteria relating to the decision process itself is applicable, simply because there would be little or no past experience to provide an historical measure.

15

Where existing organisations are being considered it is probably best to accept such historical evidence at face value. Accepting it and being satisfied with the situation are two different things. If it is possible it would be wise to institute some monitoring system so that future decision making by that particular person is shadowed by personnel using formal approaches. In this way it may be determined whether his decision-making process corresponds with the formal approach, in result if not detail, or whether he consistently selects better alternatives. If it is the latter the best strategy would be to double his salary and promote him!

THE RELEVANCE OF COST CONSIDERATIONS

Although cost considerations in the decision-making process have already been discussed these have mainly referred to the cost of collecting further information at a given point in time. This of course is very important although such costs are not always easy to assess. The bulk of the costs incurred may be the cost of delaying the decision or the cost of the time taken to gather the information.

However there are many other cost factors apart from these. For instance the consequence of a particular event happening when a given act is chosen is usually expressed in monetary terms. In general these financial consequences have to be estimated very often on far from perfect information. Hence errors in these estimates may result in incorrect decisions being made which will generally result in the incurring of costs or loss of potential profits. This problem may be obviated partially by allowing these estimates to vary within likely ranges and testing the decision model for its sensitivity to variation in these estimates. This may pinpoint areas which need exploring further.

In the practical business problem it will often be necessary to decide not to carry out an evaluation or major market research study, because it is considered that the expense is not warranted by the problem. It is inevitable that decision making at this level should become more intuitive and subjective—after all it is only the major problems, where a mistake can be very costly, that can really justify intensive studies. In addition if the problem is simple it may readily be dealt with in a purely subjective manner.

The cost considerations are of paramount importance. Where the decision alternatives are of serious consequence then it is probably worth spending a considerable sum for more certain information but for less important decisions it is not worth the expense. Just where the boundary lies is difficult to say— probably it will vary from company to company and person to person according to the level of risk they are prepared to accept and their resources.

If a company has a record of successful performance, reflected in its profitability, then it may be justified in taking risks that another company should not. A company that has shown a static or declining record for a number of years might develop, as a result of spin-off, a product which is outside its present field of activity. Clearly the completion of its development, tooling and marketing could involve considerable costs which would seriously affect the company if the product turned out to be false. Since the product is outside their field of experience the company has to acquire the necessary expertise. This expertise can be acquired slowly by recruitment or quickly by acquisition. The choice will probably be to make an acquisition so that adequate marketing facilities are obtained as well.

Since the product is a new innovation it must be marginal to the acquired company itself. This means that the acquired company must be evaluated primarily on the basis of its existing products and hence the decision which is facing the management is whether to take a major strategic step into another field. If they are in a weak financial position the last thing which should be considered is a major diversification into another field, at least not without rationalising their present organisation. Hence their decision should be to either discontinue development of the product or to sell it to a company already in that field if possible. Unfortunately the usual case is that the management are often gripped by 'new technology fever' and see the new development as an opportunity to get their company moving again.

If the company is in a really bad spot it may be that the only thing that will save them is a 'long shot' coming up. This is all right providing it is recognised that it is a 'long shot'.

MARKETING DECISION MAKING WITHIN THE OVER-ALL ORGANISATION

Although decision making is extremely important, there are other aspects of marketing which are equally important. Administration and getting the proposed solution to a problem properly implemented are of prime importance. In the extreme case it is of no consequence that good decisions are made if these are not put into practice. For example, if it is decided on rational grounds—that is demand/cost considerations—that a particular product line must be axed, then an internal side effect may be that part of the sales force has to be made redundant.

This could set up opposition amongst the remaining sales personnel who may see the situation as a clear threat to their own future security. They may take all manner of actions which could adversely affect the company. Hence some steps should be taken to evaluate the consequences of the various actions they may take and these may be included in the formal decision analysis.

It is important to realise that the probability of a successful outcome of a specific act is conditional not only upon various events happening but also on the type of personnel who take the proposed action. Therefore it follows that successful decision making requires not only systematic and formal analysis but also the right quality of staff to carry out the proposed actions. This requirement means in turn that the organisation should have a sophisticated personnel/labour relations and intelligence network. In other words the personnel manager becomes an explicit part of the decision making process.

While it is necessary to have some ideas about how specific groups of personnel will respond in given situations, it is equally important to evaluate the management who are responsible for implementation and co-ordination. There are broadly two categories of successful administrators, with infinite variation between them. There are the 'pushers' or 'drivers' and there are the 'persuaders'. The first tend to get things done by their own drive and effort, rigorously supervising and meting out incentive and disincentive as the situation merits. They are probably more dogmatic and they completely believe in what they are doing and either inspire disciples or hatred. In the short-term they will tend to get things done faster than the persuaders but in the long-term may do considerable harm. There are examples of extremely bad labour relations in British industry today which are the legacies of a handful of drivers. Whether the short-term gains outweigh the longer term damage is probably irresolvable.

The 'persuader' on the other hand tries to obtain co-operation by explaining why certain action is being taken, and seeks to get his staff to participate more in the whole picture instead of small sections. He may also evolve systems of incentives and disincentives but he may take much longer to get something done than the 'driver'. In fact the persuader is often without considerable drive himself and can therefore hardly expect to develop it in others. He is also less likely to produce the inpenetrable resistance that the 'driver' may on occasion build up.

There are occasions when only the strongest 'driver' could possibly hope to get things done—for example the completion of a large complex contract against a tight time schedule. Equally however, there are occasions when it would be madness to allow this type of person within 100 miles of the situation— for example when negotiating for an acquisition there are often occasions when firmness has to be coupled with considerable diplomacy.

Ideally a manager would have qualities of both drive and persuasion and use whichever was required. In practice there are few really persuasive pushers and even fewer persuaders with tremendous drive. It is obvious why. A driver must by nature be impatient to get results and he knows that if he has to stop and explain every action it will cause delays. The converse is true for the other type—urgency is of secondary importance besides the job of keeping his staff happy, and maybe preserving his image as a decent fellow.

On balance it is probably the 'drivers' that achieve the most. If they have a good 'relations' man then the long-term disadvantages may not ensue. Clearly in an organisation where good information systems exist there is much more scope for the 'pusher' to achieve even better results without setting up longer term reactions.

Certainly it is likely that an organisation which encourages greater participation in its problems and affairs is likely to do well providing this does not slow up the whole administrative machinery. Again if the information system is such that individual efforts are noticed and duly rewarded this should be beneficial. The largest negative factor is probably where personnel are instructed to do things and have no idea why; often things that on the surface appear to be inconsequential, and sometimes are, and therefore not worth doing. If, in addition, sustained efforts are seen to have no more impact than the casual approach, because of the absence of feedback, it will not be long before the organisation becomes tired and lethargic.

Another important aspect of the marketing manager's responsibilities is formulating longer term strategies. For example working within the bounds of corporate objectives, how he may improve his market share for a given product. At this level of responsibility there should almost certainly be some interplay between him and the management services organisation. For more important strategic considerations, for example discontinuing a product line, the decision must be made with reference to the central function.

The information and communication function of the marketing manager gives him responsibility to ensure an adequate flow of information both to his own board and back to the central departments and also from these back down to his sales managers and salesmen. He is responsible for part of the company's intelligence network simply because his staff are in constant touch with the market. They should feed back customer and competitor information as well as estimating the probability of getting business or winning contracts. In return they should receive processed information to help them sell more effectively and to see the results of their efforts.

The salesman has to execute the orders which the sales manager gives him and sell in the areas which are allocated to him. He may be instructed as to how he should go about the job of selling, but he will still need to make decisions continuously, often on the spur of the moment. To help him to do this, he needs to be completely familiar with the products he is selling, aware of the factors which motivate his potential customers, and knowledgeable of current market changes and competitive activity including comparative prices.

All this 'briefing' type information should be generated by the marketing manager and, of course, be continuously modified by the information the salesman feeds back. It follows that the information feedback function is very important simply because the salesman is always operating in the market and should be able to discern changes in the atmosphere before most other people.

Further, if he is involved in demand forecasting—by submitting estimates of the probability with which he thinks specific orders will be obtained, it is essential that any other market information which is obtained from elsewhere in the organisation is allowed to flow to him. For example, if a market research study is carried out the relevant results should be given to the salesmen.

Although the salesman is of course concerned primarily with the physical act of selling and is often motivated by having explicit targets to beat, the information feedback activities mentioned are important. It is likely that the best salesmen are those who have built up their own information systems. Their performance can probably be improved by building up a formal intelligence system. This would be the case even if the salesman spent a little less time on selling and a little more time on fact finding. If the overall organisation is to benefit, more effort should be made to get the salesman's information on to official record so that it can be used if necessary in the decision-making process.

This last point applies right through the organisation. However, it may not be accomplished in many cases without considerable opposition since the strength of an individual is often his own personal information system. In fact most organisations probably have employees who only survive because they have information sources which are not generally known about or not usually available. A striking example is the 'old boy' network which operates at various levels. It is difficult to know how this sort of intelligence system can be incorporated into a formal system. It is even more difficult to provide a method of evaluating the worth of information from these informal sources. One extreme example of how misleading these sources can be on occasions relates to a market estimate in lithographic printing. Three years before, a very rough survey had been carried out by a company with little knowledge of research methods and it was openly admitted, at the time, that the results were only a guide to the true position. A summary of the results included an estimate of the proportion that lithography was of the total market.

Another company with interests in this field was trying to answer roughly the same question three years after the survey had been carried out. Its research personnel did not know of the survey but learnt from a trade association that the proportion was x per cent. This was confirmed by various experts in the industry. It was not until much later that the researcher came across a reference to the survey carried out earlier. He then realised that the estimates he had obtained all stemmed from the same source and that if this were wrong, the evidence he had so painfully built up was invalid.

This example emphasises the dangers in obtaining independent market estimates and forming a conclusion when several such estimates are the same. One way to guard against the dangers is to attempt to get from the experts the source of their information so that these sources may be checked if possible. Considerable caution should always be exercised whenever important decisions rest to some extent on expert opinion. Needless to say, however, many examples could be given where expert estimates are very useful.

CHAPTER 10

Conclusion

THE PRACTICAL APPLICATION OF SCIENTIFIC METHODS TO BUSINESS PROBLEMS

The body of techniques and the approach outlined in this text can be considered as constituting part of what is termed management science. Some people, maybe scientists in particular, may argue that it is quite incorrect to use the label 'science' and support their argument by reference to the inexact nature of management and its problems and possibly by the absence of general laws or principles. The criticism about the inexact nature of management problems hardly holds because even the physical sciences are at least partially inexact. The criticism regarding general laws may be more valid although it is possible to specify general principles under concisely stated conditions, which is not so different from the physical sciences.

Even if there is some substance in the above arguments against using the label science, there can surely be no general criticism against using scientific methods. After all, the manager faced with a business problem may go through the same routine as the scientist. He may use his experience and judgement to formulate some hypothesis, or make intuitive guesses. He may then make some observations and test his hypotheses. Following this he may conduct some experiment or investigation and test his hypotheses further. He will carry on this process until he is happy that the probability of the hypothesis being true is above a specific level. He may go further and get colleagues to examine his work or go through the same process or use other approaches. He may never get a scientific law because, by definition, the scientific law must have an extremely high probability of being true and further be applicable in a general way.

It is pointless discussing business problems and situations by reference to scientific laws but undoubtedly the systematic approaches that transformed the art of medicine into medical science must be applicable to the art of business.

Some considerable time has been used in discussing probability, forecasting and information systems. However a vast field of methods and their applications has been omitted. For example although sensitivity analysis has been mentioned it has not been explored in depth. Similarly the bodies of simulation techniques, games theory applications, linear and dynamic programming have not been mentioned.

Yet there are practical applications for even the most advanced techniques and it may not be possible to find the optimum solution to a particular problem without using the right technique. All the same the technique is not all important. The management scientist should certainly have a wide knowledge of specialised techniques, but he should also have a keen logical and analytical mind and in addition experience in the relevant field or industry. Each of these qualities is of the utmost importance.

The point is that providing the analyst has the right qualities then the systematic approach outlined in the preceding chapters should enable him to become more effective and make mistakes less often. Right qualities include an objective outlook and some understanding of the probabilistic nature of things.

These qualities are often combined into the thought process which determines the quality of judgements being made. It is of course difficult to distinguish clearly between intuition and judgement. At the extremes it is easy because intuition becomes a guess in the dark or a feeling in the bones, whereas judgement is the result of some logical thought process. The distinction is probably one of degree. In other words whereas judgement may best be considered as being formed on the basis of tangible evidence, intuition may be applicable where information is very sparse or where the decision maker is unable or not prepared to make full use of the information available.

It follows that even if as thorough a scientific approach as possible is used, if the decision maker is just unable to get enough evidence he may be forced to make guesses. In general the intuitive approach ought to be avoided as far as possible.

The last point is that using the scientific approach the decision maker is more likely to learn from his past experience or even better from the past experiences of others. In whatever way problems are handled some learning must follow but to maximise the amount learnt it is necessary to follow a systematic approach with some kind of feedback mechanism. However good the system developed may be, it is always possible to improve it and the decision maker should consciously endeavour to improve his performance.

A PREDICTION OF THE WAY AHEAD

It is inevitable that a text on predicting and decision making should include its own assessment of the direction in which these topics are likely to proceed. To make such an assessment it is of course necessary to form a view of the overall environment within which decision making will be required.

In the mid-term, say five to ten year period, the continued industrial rationalisation will probably be accompanied by increasing the management services function. Economists, statisticians, analysts, operations researchers will be required in increasing numbers to set up information systems, to institute decision analysis procedures and to construct models of the companies' operations. It is likely that model building as an aid to decision making will become an increasingly important requirement and considerable effort is likely to be extended in this direction.

The trend is likely to be towards setting up management service departments which will be integrated with computer departments, to provide a comprehensive internal information system. Later the information system will include externally derived information—that is by marketing researchers within the management service function and from personnel such as salesmen on a feedback basis. Work will continue on model building and decision analysis, but the main advances will come when the information systems are functioning properly.

The longer term detailed requirements are obviously difficult to assess, but it is possible to consider possible futures that may exist in ten years time. For example the present trend of industrial rationalisation in the formation of larger groups of companies is likely to continue at least as rapidly as at present for the whole of this period or even longer. By that time, if the present pace is indeed continued, there is likely to be a relatively small number of extremely large corporations operating internationally and accounting for a large proportion of the world's production and other industrial requirements. Although there will continue to be a large number of small organisations, these will tend to account for a very small proportion of total output and individual companies will be swallowed up by the larger corporations as soon as the small company grows to a moderate size.

The large corporations are likely to operate along industrial segments and the multi-industry conglomerate may be forced into extinction. This will tend to lead to faster technological growth and hence the rate of innovation will probably increase.

Since such corporations will be organised on an international basis, communications and information flow becomes a vital factor. Corporate control is likely to shift closer to the centre and fully computerised information systems would be necessary to deal with the complex information requirements of the central management. It is thought that visual outputs and video-phone systems will improve to the point that executive travel will not be required to the extent that it is today. This trend towards a more impersonal system may have adverse sociological consequences if wider participation in the decision processes is not permitted.

It is suggested therefore that decisions by central management will be made openly. By using their complex information network they can keep all the relevant employees informed as progress is made towards reaching a particular decision. Further the views of the employees may be put forward and taken into account.

Eventually the core of the corporation will almost certainly be a powerful computer system which is not only used for locating, sorting and disseminating relevant information, but also used for analysis as required. The position may be reached where the company has a large library of its own programs and the decision maker may select a decision program and feed in his own subjective probability estimates. He may then adjust these in the light of further information that the computer produces or the computer may adjust them itself.

In particular it is likely that comprehensive decision analysis programs, probably using Bayesian inference methods, will develop and these will choose the best decision alternative on financial grounds within the constraints imposed by management. Management's function may then be to assess the worth of accepting this alternative having regard to the existing sociological conditions.

There are a number of occurrences, sociological and political, which could happen and, if they do, industrial progress may not proceed this way. However, given that present trends continue there is no reason why the supra-national organisation should not eventually become primarily concerned with meeting the needs of the people who use its products and those of its employees, rather than as now where the primary concern is with making increasing levels of profits and beating its competitors. The large corporations, by breaking down national political and religious barriers, could conceivably become the world's best vehicles for preserving peace and prosperity, not just for those countries which are industrialised at present but for the whole world.

By increasing automation of production there should be considerable leisure time for people to pursue more creative activities. Work may then constitute just that proportion of his total time that is acceptable to the individual.

Such a future is obtainable and if it were generally regarded as being the type of future that should be sought then the action which is taken today will have some bearing on its occurrence or not.

Mathematical Appendix

Reference 1. Chapter 3 Page 68
Mathematical representation of the additive series time model

If the demand for a product in period i is denoted Y_i and if $\hat{Y}_t$ represents the estimated demand in this period then the moving average denoted M_t is calculated from

$$M_t = 1/n\,[Y_t + Y_{t-1} + \ldots + Y_{t-n+1}]$$

where n is the number of periods in the average. M_t therefore corresponds with a point approximately $n/2$ periods away.

If S_i is the seasonal component in period i and C_i is the cyclical component in period i and T_i is the trend component in period i then the model is written down as follows

$$\hat{Y}_t = T_i + S_i + C_i + E_i$$

(where E_i is a component representing random fluctuations).

Reference 2. Chapter 3 Page 71
Mathematical representation of the multiplicative time series model

Using the same notation as before this model can be written down as follows

$$\hat{Y}_t = T_i \times S_i \times C_i \times E_i$$

and
$$M_t = 1/n\,(Y_t + \ldots + Y_{t-n+1})$$

Reference 3. Chapter 3 Page 72
Mathematical representation of the exponentially smoothed moving average model

Denoting demand in period i by Y_i and the estimated demand in that period by $\hat{Y}_i$; the moving average is denoted M_t and the weight used is denoted a.

The moving average M_t is calculated by weighting the successive terms of the series subject to the sum of the weights equalling 1.

Hence

$$M_t = a\,[Y_t + (1 - a)\,Y_{t-1} + (1 - a)^2\,Y_{t-2} + \ldots + (1 - a)^n\,Y_{t-n}]$$

and

$$M_{t-1} = a\,[Y_{t-1} + (1 - a)\,Y_{t-2} + (1 - a)^2\,Y_{t-3} + \ldots + (1 - a)_{n-1}\,Y_{t-n}]$$

$$\therefore\ M_t = a\,[Y_t + \frac{(M_{t-1})\,(1 - a)}{2}] = a\,Y_t + (1 - a)\,M_{t-1}$$

Hence

$$M_t = M_{t-1} + a\,(Y_t + M_{t-1})$$

If r_t is the trend value in period t then the model may be represented by

$$M_t = aY_t + (1 - a)\,[M_{t-1} + r_{t-1}]$$

and if

$$E_t = Y_t - (M_{t-1} + r_{t-1})$$

then

$$M_t = (M_{t-1} + r_{t-1}) + aE_t$$

where E_t is the random variable in period t.

Reference 4. Chapter 3 Page 77
The linear trend model

Denoting demand in period T_i as Y_i then a linear equation is fitted to the pairs of values (Y, T), of the form

$$\hat{Y} = a + bT$$

where $\hat{Y}$ is the estimate of Y and a and b are parameters estimated by least squares, T_i takes the values 1 to N.

a may be regarded as the intercept of the line—that is where the line crosses the vertical axis; and b is the slope of the line—that is the angle it makes with the horizontal axis.

The way in which a and b are estimated is described in detail in chapter 7, pages 174–175.

The formulae required are

$$b = \frac{\displaystyle\sum_{i=1}^{N} (T_i - \bar{T})(Y_i - \bar{Y})}{\Sigma (T_i - \bar{T})^2}$$

for all pairs of Y_i and T_i and a is calculated from

$$a = \bar{Y} - b\bar{T}$$

where $\bar{Y}$ and $\bar{T}$ are the means of the Y_i and T_i respectively.

If the two variables are taken as deviations from their respective means then denoting these y_i' and t_i'

$$y_i' = Y_i - \bar{Y} \text{ and } t_i' = T_i - \bar{T}$$

The formula for b can then be written more simply as

$$b = \frac{\Sigma (y \; t_i')}{\Sigma (t_i')^2}$$

and a is calculated as before.

The standard deviation of regression is a measure of how well the calculated line fits the actual data. To calculate this, each of the estimated values of Y are subtracted from the actual value for that period. These differences are squared and then added together. The sum obtained is divided by the number of periods minus two, to obtain the mean sum of squares.

The square root of the value so obtained is the standard deviation of regression.

If we denote the differences by E_t then this set of events can be written down as

$$E_1 = Y_1 - \hat{Y}_1; E_2 = Y_2 - \hat{Y}_2; \ldots E_N = Y_N - \hat{Y}_N$$

and $E_1{}^2 = (Y_1 - \hat{Y}_1)^2; E_2{}^2 = (Y_2 - \hat{Y}_2)^2; \ldots E_N = (Y_N - \hat{Y}_N)^2$

hence $E_1{}^2 + E_2{}^2 + \ldots + E_N{}^2 = (Y_1 - \hat{Y}_1)^2 +$

$$(Y_2 - \hat{Y}_2)^2 + \ldots + (Y_N - \hat{Y}_N)^2$$

or $\displaystyle\sum_i^N E_t{}^2 = \sum^N (Y_i - Y_i)^2$

16

and the mean sum of squares is

$$\frac{\sum\limits_{i}^{N} E_i^2}{N-2} = \frac{\sum\limits_{i}^{N} (Y_i - \hat{Y}_i)^2}{N-2}$$

and the standard deviation is the square root of this

$$\sqrt{\frac{\sum\limits_{i}^{N} E_i^2}{N-2}} \text{ or } \sqrt{\frac{\sum\limits_{i}^{N} (Y_i - Y_i)^2}{N-2}}$$

A prediction for Y given, say, the value $(T + r)$ is obtained by substituting $(T + r)$ in the equation.

Reference 5. Chapter 3 Page 78
Fitting the logistic curve using the three point method

In this method three averages are calculated, the first for the first $N/3$ periods, the second for the second $N/3$ periods and the third for the last $N/3$ periods.

If these three averages are denoted by R, S and T respectively then a, b and r are calculated from the following formulae

$$(\log r) \times \left[\frac{N - N/3}{2}\right] = \log \left[\frac{T - S}{S - R}\right] ;$$

$$\log r = \frac{2}{N - N/3} \times \log \left[\frac{S - R}{T - S}\right] ;$$

$$a = \frac{S^2 - TR}{2S - T - R}$$

$$\text{and } b = \frac{N/3}{(r + r^2 + r^3 + \ldots)} \times \frac{(S - R)^2}{2S - T - R}$$

Reference 6. Chapter 4 Page 108
The standard error of an estimate made from a regression equation

Reference 4 showed that the standard deviation of regression for the equation

$$\hat{Y} = a + bT$$

is $$\sqrt{\dfrac{\overset{N}{\underset{i}{\Sigma}} (Y_t - \hat{Y}_t)^2}{N - 2}} = \sigma$$

This formula applies whatever variable is considered on the right-hand side of the linear equation—that is time or any other independent variable (X).

The standard error of the estimate of Y given a specific value of X—that is $\hat{Y}|X_k$ is calculated from the formulae:

$$\sigma\hat{Y} = \sqrt{\left\{ \dfrac{\sigma^2}{N}\left[1 + N + N\dfrac{(X_k - \overline{X})^2}{(X_t - X)^2} \right] \right\}}$$

Reference 7. Chapter 6 Page 135
The addition law of probabilities

If the probability of event A occurring is $P(A)$ and the probability of event B occurring is $P(B)$ then if the two events A and B are mutually exclusive—that is if one occurs then the other cannot—the probability of either one or the other occurring is simply

$$P[A + B] = P(A) + P(B)$$

In the case of a coin, the probability of a head being thrown in one toss is $P(H) = \frac{1}{2}$ and the probability of a tail is $P(T) = \frac{1}{2}$. Since one of these events must occur and both cannot, then the probability that either a head or a tail is thrown is

$$P(H) + P(T) = \tfrac{1}{2} + \tfrac{1}{2} = 1$$

that is certainty.

In the case of throwing a die once, there are six possible events, 1, 2, 3, 4, 5 or 6 and the probability of each is $\frac{1}{6}$.

Hence, from the addition law, the probability of throwing in one toss a 1 or a 2 is

$$P(1) + P(2) = \tfrac{1}{6} + \tfrac{1}{6} = \tfrac{1}{3}$$

Suppose however that event A represents the occurrence of an odd number in one throw of the die—that is a 1 or a 3 or a 5. Suppose further that event B represents a number under 5.

The results of a throw can be written down as

Class A (odd numbers)	Class B (numbers under 5)	Other results
1	1	6
3	2	
5	3	
	4	

Clearly the application of the law of addition of probabilities described before, to the probability that either event A or event B occurs gives

$$P(A + B) = P(A) + P(B) = \tfrac{1}{2} + \tfrac{2}{3} = 7/6$$

Since this result is equivalent to saying the probability of throwing an odd number or a number less than 5 is more than certainty, the law is obviously wrong in this case.

The fault is in fact that the two events A and B are not mutually exclusive—for example if an ace is thrown it belongs to both the class A and the class B. Therefore an adjustment has to be made for this 'double counting'.

The probability of a result occurring which belongs to class A is

$$P(A) = P(1) + P(3) + P(5) = \tfrac{1}{6} + \tfrac{1}{6} + \tfrac{1}{6} = \tfrac{1}{2}$$

The probability of a result occurring which belongs to class B is

$$P(B) = P(1) + P(2) + P(3) + P(4) = \tfrac{1}{6} + \tfrac{1}{6} + \tfrac{1}{6} + \tfrac{1}{6} = \tfrac{2}{3}$$

Both the throwing of a 1 or a 3 are common to both classes and hence $\tfrac{1}{6} + \tfrac{1}{6} = \tfrac{1}{3}$ must be deducted from $P(A) + P(B)$.

That is,

$$P(A) \quad + \quad P(B) \quad - \quad P(AB)$$
$$= (\tfrac{1}{6} + \tfrac{1}{6} + \tfrac{1}{6}) + (\tfrac{1}{6} + \tfrac{1}{6} + \tfrac{1}{6} + \tfrac{1}{6}) - (\tfrac{1}{6} + \tfrac{1}{6})$$
$$= \quad \tfrac{1}{2} \quad + \quad \tfrac{4}{6} \quad - \quad \tfrac{2}{6} \quad = \quad \tfrac{5}{6}$$

More formally the term $P(AB)$ represents the probability of both event A and event B occurring together—that is $\tfrac{1}{2} \times \tfrac{2}{3}$.

In the general case, if there are two events A and B having probabilities of occurring of $P(A)$ and $P(B)$ respectively, then the probability that at least one of these occurs is 1 minus the probability that they both fail to occur.

Since the probability of each occurring is $P(A)$ and $P(B)$

then the probability that each fails to occur is $1 - P(A)$ and $1 - P(B)$ respectively.

Hence the probability that they both fail to occur is

$$[1 - P(A)] \times [1 - P(B)]$$

Therefore the probability that at least one of the two events occurs is

$$\begin{aligned} P(A + B) &= 1 - \left\{ [1 - P(A)][1 - P(B)] \right\} \\ &= 1 - [1 - P(A) - P(B) + P(A)\,P(B)] \\ &= P(A) + P(B) - P(A)\,P(B) \end{aligned}$$

In the die example $P(A) = \frac{1}{2}$ and $P(B) = \frac{1}{3}$ and hence the probability of either an odd number or a number under 5 is

$$\begin{aligned} P(A + B) &= P(A) + P(B) - P(A)\,P(B) \\ &= \tfrac{1}{2} + \tfrac{2}{3} - \tfrac{1}{2} \times \tfrac{2}{3} \\ &= 7/6 - \tfrac{2}{6} = \tfrac{5}{6} \end{aligned}$$

The addition law of probabilities can be extended to cover as many events as required. For example for the three events A, B and C having probabilities $P(A)$, $P(B)$ and $P(C)$ the same argument gives:

$$\begin{aligned} P(A + B + C) &= 1 - \left\{ [1 - P(A)][1 - P(B)][1 - P(C)] \right\} \\ &= 1 - \left\{ 1 - P(A) - P(B) - P(C) \right. \\ &\quad + P(A)P(B) + P(A)P(C) \\ &\quad + P(B)P(C) - P(A)P(B)P(C) \left. \right\} \\ &= P(A) + P(B) + P(C) - P(A)P(B) \\ &\quad - P(A)P(C) - P(B)P(C) \\ &\quad + P(A)P(B)P(C) \end{aligned}$$

If $P(A) = P(B) = P(C)$ then

$$P(A + B + C) = 3P(A) - 3[P(A)]^2 + [P(A)]^3$$

This is the sort of expression used in the pricing and bidding model, p. 162.

Reference 8. Chapter 6 Page 135
The multiplication law of probability

Using the same notation as in reference 7 the probability of both events A and B occurring together was shown to be

$$P(AB) = P(A) \times P(B) = \tfrac{2}{3} \times \tfrac{1}{2} = \tfrac{1}{3}$$

Suppose B is known to have occurred—that is the result of the throw is a number under 5, but exactly which value is not known, then the event A can happen in only two ways—that is an ace or a three.

If the probability of A in this situation is written $P(A|B)$—that is the probability that A occurs given that B has, then

$$P(A|B) = \frac{\text{Number of events corresponding with A and B}}{\text{Number of events corresponding with B only}}$$

$$= \frac{\text{ace or three}}{\text{ace, two, three or four}} = 2/4 = \tfrac{1}{2}$$

In symbols this is $P(A|B) = P(AB)/P(B)$.

Hence $P(AB) = P(A|B) \times P(B) = \tfrac{1}{2} \times \tfrac{2}{3} = \tfrac{2}{6} = \tfrac{1}{3}$.

If $P(A)B$ is the same as $P(A)$ as it is in this case then the event B is said to be statistically independent of event A and

$$P(AB) = P(A) \times P(B)$$

For independent events, the joint probability of them all occurring is

$$P(A) \times P(B) \times P(C) \times \ldots \times P(N)$$

The symbolic statement $P(AB) = P(B) P(A|B)$ is the same as saying that the probability of both events A and B occurring simultaneously equals the probability that B occurs alone and that A occurs given that B has already occurred.

For the case of three events A, B and C having probabilities $P(A)$, $P(B)$ and $P(C)$ respectively, the multiplication law either yields

$$P(ABC) = P(A) P(B) P(C)$$

where A, B and C are independent; or

$$P(ABC) = P(A) P(B|A) P(C|AB)$$

where they are not.

The latter expression is proved as follows. Since $P(AB) = P(A) P(B|A)$ then denoting the combined event (AB) by the label X, it follows that

$$P(XC) = P(X) \, P(C|X) = P(A) \, P(B|A) \, P(C|X)$$

or

$$P(ABC) = P(A) \, P(B|A) \, P(C|AB)$$

This result can be generalised for as many results as are required.

Reference 9. Chapter 6 Page 136
The conditional law of probability

The concept of conditional probability—$P(B|A)$—was required in the development of the multiplication law of probability.

As an example, consider the probability of throwing an ace in one throw of a die if it is known that an odd number had already occurred.

The marginal probability of throwing an ace, called event A is $P(A) = \frac{1}{6}$.

However, since the result is known to be odd then the face showing can only be either an ace, a three or a five. If the event 'odd number' is denoted by B then the probability of an ace given that B has occurred is

$$P(A|B) = \tfrac{1}{3}$$

This is simply because the total number of cases has been restricted to three and one must occur. In symbols

$$P(A|B) = \frac{P(AB)}{P(B)} = \frac{\frac{1}{6}}{\frac{1}{2}} = \tfrac{1}{3}$$

Note that $P(AB)$ is $\frac{1}{6}$ in this case because there is only one way in which both events A and B can occur—that is if an ace is thrown.

If $B_1, B_2, \ldots, B_N$ is a set of mutually exclusive events of which one necessarily occurs then event A can only occur in conjunction with one of the Bs.

In logical symbols

$$A = AB_1 \cup AB_2 \cup \ldots \cup AB_N$$

where $\cup$ is the logical symbol meaning either—that is the union of A and B.

Hence

$$P(A) = P(AB_1) \cup P(AB_2) \ldots \cup P(AB_N)$$
$$= \Sigma\, P[A|B_i]P(B_i)$$

Reference 10. Chapter 6 Page 142
Bayesian Probability

Bayes Theorem
Consider the event B that never occurs unless it is preceded by one or other of the set of events A_i, each of which is mutually exclusive. If it is known that B has occurred, the probability that it was preceded by a particular one of the As is calculable. This is the product of the unconditional probability of that specific A and the probability of it being followed by event B, expressed as a ratio of all such combinations.

If $P(A_1)\ P(A_2) \ldots P(A_N)$ are the probabilities of events $A_1, A_2, \ldots, A_N$ occurring, these are the prior probabilities.

The posterior probability, $P(A_k|B)$ is required

$$P(A_k|B) = P(A_k)\ P(B|A_k) = P(B)\ P(A_k|B)$$
$$P(A_k)\ P(B|A_k) = P(B)\ P(A_k|B)$$

and

$$P(A_k|B) = \frac{P(A_k)\ P(B|A_k)}{P(B)} \qquad (1)$$

If the As are exhaustive then

$$P(A|B_1) + P(A_2|B) + \ldots + P(A_N|B) = 1$$

Hence

$$\frac{P(A_1)\ P(B|A_1)}{P(B)} + \frac{P(A_2)\ P(B|A_2)}{P(B)} + \ldots = 1$$

Hence from equation (1)

$P(A_k|B)$

$$= \frac{P(A_k)P(B|A_k)}{P(A_1)P(B|A_1) + P(A_2)P(B|A_2) + \ldots + P(A_N)P(B\ A_N)}$$

$$= \frac{P(A_k)P(B|A_k)}{\overset{N}{\Sigma}\, P(A_i)P(B|A_i)}$$

Index